AMBITIOUS ADVENTURES *in* Organic Farming

AMBITIOUS ADVENTURES *in* Organic Farming

Joanne White

BIG MOOSE PUBLISHING

Published by: Big Moose Publishing
PO Box 127 Site 601 RR#6 Saskatoon, SK CANADA S7K3J9
www.bigmoosepublishing.com

Printed in Canada.

ISBN: 978-1-989840-29-0 (soft cover)
ISBN: 978-1-989840-30-6 (e-book)

Big Moose Publishing 10/2021

For Jimmy, the Real Deal

TABLE OF CONTENTS

PART 1

Sheeping

It's March – a brutally cold time of year on our farm, which is nestled between the small towns of Lumsden and Regina Beach in Saskatchewan. There is still a good layer of snow on the ground. Such weather has necessitated a vigilance in watching our pregnant ewes to be sure they don't drop a tiny, wet, newborn lamb onto snow-laden, frozen ground.

Our flock of sheep came to us from a neighbouring farm. It consisted of thirty ewes and one very proud ram who'd done his duty (with all thirty of them prior to their arrival on our farm).

While horses and cows (and probably anything else that is bigger than me) make me nervous, I actually rather like sheep. Their version of aggression seems to be an enthusiastic stampede towards the promise of food, swiftly followed by a nervous retreat, if there turns out to be no food on offer after all. They have a sort of part-time fear of humans.

We've had sheep before. Two farms ago we had a small flock which Jimmy endeavoured to shear single-handedly, while I stood on the sidelines with a bottle of iodine at the ready for the inevitable cuts and nicks. After the first sheep, he decided he would never attempt shearing again with sweat pouring from everywhere and a wriggling ewe that had spent well over half an hour determined to escape his stockinged-feet grasp. But, after the twelfth and final sheep, a misplaced form of victorious confidence took hold, a lot like that endorphin high at the end of a gruelling 26-mile marathon where a triumphant runner believes he could "do it all again tomorrow." Jimmy decided the whole ordeal was a conquest to be not only celebrated, but also most certainly repeated!

But this time, it wasn't an intense afternoon of shearing; it was more than a month of lambing. For those who aren't familiar, lambing is caring for pregnant ewes and watching over them to ensure the lambs are born safely. You have to check on them day and night to make sure there are no complications.

No doubt the seasoned shepherd will raise an eyebrow and call me a lightweight, but I find the midnight vigils combined with the 5:00am vigils to be utterly exhausting. I only did this twice. It is Jimmy who does the lion's share of ewe-watching, with late nights, midnights, and dark o'clocks in the mornings, right on the heels of his regular school-bus driving job.

Some of our darlings have done a fine job of birthing all by themselves, cleaning up baby and successfully nursing with nary a midwife nor La Leche League advisor in sight. Others not so much.

Our first casualty was a second lamb of twins. Mrs. Ewe delivered the first just fine one evening, and seemed to be quite settled. Jimmy made the erroneous assumption that it was a single birth.

That morning, Jimmy began his rounds as usual at about 5:00am. He went out and milked the cow, gave hay to the cattle, came in for breakfast and our very English pot of tea, and then headed out on his school bus run. I also did my usual morning rounds which involved me rallying our four children, who still lived at home and attended the local grade schools.

Once Jimmy returned from his bus route, we tackled the remaining farm chores together, which, at that time of year, included food rations of mixed grains and hay (all organic, of course) for all our livestock, depending on who they were and what they needed, and any required water top-ups.

We noticed our mama had no interest in her grain, which is a big indication that all was not well in her world. As Jimmy continued his feeding rounds in the barn, I stood and watched her for a while. She was decidedly not settled any more.

A neighbour visited with a wealth of sheepy experience of his own. That's when we realized she had been pregnant with twins and hadn't delivered the second, now dead, lamb.

Between the two men, a good portion of the morning was spent trying to remove it. It is a sad thing to see something so small and lifeless. Jimmy felt terrible that he hadn't checked more thoroughly the previous evening, but there was nothing to be done to change it.

I delivered the carcass to the pigs.

It may seem awful and heartless, but we couldn't bury our dead lamb; the ground was still frozen. I also didn't want to dump our dead lamb in the perimeter bushes, because it would attract predators. Since pigs are omnivorous, they could make use of the nutrition imparted to our dead lamb over the course of Mrs. Ewe's pregnancy. It would help the pigs who hadn't found many grubs to scavenge since the big freeze, and it would successfully process a lost lamb into a combination of pork-building nutrients and soil-feeding manure. I saw it as a win-win. Truly, our hearts knew this to be the best course for all involved.

The next casualty was Mrs. Ewe herself. With no antibiotics onhand right away, it was later that day when Jimmy returned from the vet with a bottle and some needles.

Mrs. Ewe was managing very poorly and our two youngest daughters, ever eager to bottle feed the newborn, fed her surviving lamb with milk replacement feeds throughout the day. Fifteen minutes after her first shot of antibiotics, Mrs. Ewe turned her toes up and breathed her last breath.

Our lovely neighbour offered to come and butcher her for us, but those antibiotics imposed a "safe withdrawal period" before recommending human consumption of meat. So, I delivered her carcass to the pigs as well.

With all that wool, I felt the pigs would need a bit of help to feed on her. I took our sharpest serrated carving knife, and slit her open from throat to udder, allowing the pigs unhindered access to her internal organs. You may think it was gross and disgusting, but I am all for that Circle of Life thinking. No one ever said farming was glamorous.

With many weeks to go until the pigs faced their own slaughter, the antibiotics would be long gone after their feasting.

Jimmy nicknamed me Big Butcher.

Dealing with dead bodies was not new to me. Many moons ago, I worked in a teaching mortuary in Manchester, England, that accepted human body donations or 'bequeathals,' as they were called. Some years were lean pickings in terms of body donations and my colleague at the time would make Burke and Hare jokes about us "goin' out an' doin' a bit o' killin' over t'weekend" (he was a Yorkshireman) to improve the supplies for our resident doctors, dentists, surgeons, podiatrists, and paramedics. Conversely, some years yielded an abundance of body donations and we had what I can only politely refer to as "left-overs".

I was relatively new to my post, and I suspect my then-boss had Machiavellian motives to test my mettle when he handed me a surgical hacksaw (which is exactly the same as a regular hacksaw but made entirely of stainless steel for sterilization purposes – a moot point in a mortuary) and a scalpel to make two intact bodies fit into each of their standard-sized receptacles (a 20-gallon round plastic bin). At that time in my life, I had not come into the faith I would find in later years. Nonetheless, I had a profound respect for the dead and wished their departed human-ness complete peace as I began the process of careful, but purposeful, dismembering.

Jimmy knows this story. I am not a butcher in the hacking and slashing sense, but I am prepared to do what needs to be done in situations such as these.

With lambing season still in full swing, it wasn't too many days later that another Mrs. Ewe had a face at both ends. Jimmy watched and waited, but that little face didn't make much progress. Hot water, soap, and oodles of time later, the biggest lamb imaginable was plopped next to its mama's head for cleaning. This time the second lamb was a breeze, and slid itself out without a single glitch.

Mrs. Ewe was very concerned for her first born giant, and began to reject the second twin. First Born couldn't stand up, even with larger-than-normal legs. She had no apparent shoulder damage; she just couldn't get up. Our two youngest daughters, still ever eager to bottle feed newborn lambs, diligently brought First Born feed after feed, each gratefully received with enthusiasm. But poor Second Twin was getting bunted away, and not allowed to suckle from its mum.

By the second day, First Born had developed some wheezing, and by the third day, she was dead. Big Butcher carved her up and delivered her to the pigs. On the plus side, Second Twin was now being accepted, and we no longer needed to supplement her, much to our daughters' disappointment.

While all this drama was playing out in one pen (called a 'jug' in Farmer-Speak), another drama was playing out in the next. A third Mrs. Ewe also had twins, delivered successfully and lovingly cleaned. The only problem was she had no udder to speak of, and her poor children hunted and bleated in vain to find their first meal.

Again, our two youngest daughters came to the rescue, bottle feeding just enough to give them strength, but not enough to make them lose interest in their mama. Jimmy, wearing the hat of La Leche League advisor, milked Mrs. Ewe by hand to get things going, and pushed not-so-hungry-but-not-too-full lamb heads towards Mrs. Ewe's small udder.

A third jug simultaneously had yet another variation of sheepy drama. One strong twin was happily feeding independently, while the other was weak and shivering. No amount of coaxing or bottle feeding attempts resulted in a substantial meal for it. Weak Shivering Twin was dead the morning after the death of First Born, and she met the same Circle of Life fate at the hands of Big Butcher.

La Leche League Jimmy succeeded in stimulating lactation for Mrs. Ewe-with-the-Small-Udder. Her twins ended up doing just fine with no help from our two young disappointed daughters.

Then, we had one Mrs. Ewe who seemed to be in complete denial of having birthed her son. She ran away from him when he attempted to find milk, and she bunted him quite ferociously with her head when he came near her. She even ran right over him when we tried to intervene.

Jimmy created a separate little jug-within-a-jug for him, leaving him with his Mad Mama for just a few minutes at a time, so that he could sneak a decent feed from her, before she realized what was happening and ran away from and/or over him. It took only a couple of days for her to settle down and realize it was her own lamb.

It was a juggle to move groups of ewes down to the barn in anticipation of their lambs' arrivals, and then move groups of mums with lambs old enough to cope outside back up to the corralled area out in the field. Only a couple of times did we misjudge the two-way traffic flow, and found a newborn lamb lying in the snow in the outdoor corral, having believed mama was nowhere near ready to deliver.

One of those times we were extremely lucky that my second-oldest daughter and I arrived with the morning grain ration when we did. There we found a newborn lamb, no more than a few minutes old, but it wasn't moving and looked as though it was dead. Little did we know that our arrival with food had done nothing to help Mama Ewe stop and take the time to lick her little offspring clean and coax him into taking his first drink. She saw our buckets and simply abandoned the item that had just fallen from her rear end to go and enjoy her own breakfast!

As soon as our grain had been poured into the troughs and the other sheep were happy, I went over to take a look myself. The lamb was still tightly bound within the amniotic sac, and couldn't breathe at all. I wiped at his nose and mouth with my gloved hand, and to my absolute delight, he took a breath and began to try to wriggle his way out of the membrane that was stuck to him. He was alive!

We dashed back to the yard to fetch Jimmy and our calf-sled, a large black plastic container that had a pull-rope attached. We could use it to pull mama and baby over the snow and down to the barn.

Gathering baby was easy. He was exactly where we left him and still wrapped up in his remarkably tough membrane, which we freed him from with an old towel we had brought along and subsequently wrapped him snugly into for the short-but-cold ride. Gathering mama was a little trickier. Even spotting mama was quite difficult. How do you tell which of the chomping-at-the-trough ewes had let her tummy overrule her maternal instincts? But we deduced she was the one with all that goo hanging out of her back end.

Jimmy was fast enough to catch her, but it took the three of us to tip her onto her back into the calf sled, with her baby tucked under her nose. We made it a few yards across the snow-covered field, before her wriggling became so incessant that we just couldn't hold her still. A rope 'hobble' helped, and impeded her desire to escape just enough that we managed to make the rest of the journey. Still, my daughter and I had to take turns at the back-breaking task of holding her still. This involved walking bent over double to reach down to her and keep a firm grip. The pair were then tucked into a jug all of their own, and both made excellent progress.

Seeing the flock members returned to the corralled pasture is another success story. Snow was melting, temperatures were rising, and lambs were springing and leaping and racing around (otherwise known as "gamboling").

It was impossible not to make up dialogue for them… "Look at me! Look at me! Look how fast I can run! Look how high I can jump!" I laughed out loud when I watched Proud Ram befuddled by all these small bouncy things. I could imagine Mrs. Ewe asking, "Would you help a little and watch the children?" Proud Ram would barely lift his head from the feed trough and say, "Not my problem."

Our next Mrs. Ewe had been marked as one likely to lamb the earliest, with big udders showing right from the beginning of the month. The farming term is 'bagging up', and I have this odd image in my head of a group of construction workers whistling at a passing female shouting, "Look at the bags on that!" The term doesn't sit quite right, does it? Bagging up?…Like a 'bag lady': a lost and unfortunate soul dragging large quantities of detritus around the streets; or bags like carry-on luggage at the flight desk. But then a number of farming terms are odd, such as testicles being called 'stones', or a scrotum being called a 'purse' – yes, really! "Where's my purse?" now has a whole new meaning. But Mrs. Ewe had bags… big bags… so we were increasingly surprised as the other ewes popped out their lambs with varying degrees of ease or difficulty, while this Mrs. Ewe simply bided her time chewing her cud and resting.

Jimmy is rather tied to a schedule on school days. Of course, Mrs. Ewe decided to join the party of lamb-birthing just before the afternoon school bus run. How inconvenient of her!

Her size suggested more than one lamb. The first one came out with some help, but the second one was stuck fast. Jim pushed his departure time right to the limit, feeling he couldn't leave her for the time it took him to return home. Two front feet were out, but no head. He tried and tried to bring the lamb's head into the correct position. Each time it would simply disappear back to whatever uterine recess it was determined to occupy.

Eventually, he had no choice but to go to work. One of our sons returned home within the hour, and I persuaded him to try and help Mrs. Ewe and her lamb, a very first experience for an otherwise relatively wide-viewed and worldly-wise 16-year-old! He couldn't navigate very well and had no idea, nor much confidence in, what he was doing. I felt there was no choice but for me to try, even though I had always doggedly refused all offers from Jim to assist in the sleeves-rolled-up-way.

Whilst I am less squeamish with post-life dearly-departed specimens, I am unbelievably hesitant and nervous about dealing with *in vivo* conditions. I once tried to give an injected dose of antibiotic to a kitten with particularly gooey eyes, and the 'pop' sound that the hypodermic needle made as it went through the skin almost made me pass out. But here was this struggling ewe… and my willing-but-not-able adolescent son… I thought at least I am female and know those reproductive parts pretty well. I have personally experienced labour and delivery, at least I could generate some confidence from that.

Coat off, hands and arms scrubbed and soaped, in I went.

It was a first experience for me too! Elbow-deep in Mrs. Ewe's la-la, I began trying to find the errant head of the lamb owning those dangling front legs. I eventually found it tucked way back (imagine the crown of a head bent over enough to touch the spine!), and tried to gently pull it to the front.

Well, there's not much 'gentle' about it, if I'm honest. It is such a confined space to work in. Every time Mrs. Ewe had a contraction, I thought she might break my wrist.

Still, I refused to let that lamb's head slip back again. I had such a grip on it I felt I was squishing its eyeballs. I already believed its neck was broken. I dug my heels into the straw as I laid on one hip and pulled and pulled for all I was worth, but I could not budge that lamb.

Jimmy got back in record time. (I could just imagine him careening around each corner at top speed on just two wheels, barely slowing down at each child's stop and shouting, "Just tuck and roll!") He came to us without even turning his bus engine off. It took a while, but he got Mrs. Ewe's second, dead lamb out. I don't need to tell you where it went.

It was then towards the end of the week when Jimmy was milking our cow Daisy at 5:00am, when he heard grunting and huffing. He found Mrs. Ewe in her jug with her surviving lamb, bearing down and pushing with considerable strain. Oh no!

Still determinedly snuggled in bed (where any sane person ought to be at 5:00am in my opinion), I heard the panic in Jimmy's voice as he called my name from the open door upstairs.

Splash pants, boots, and coat were thrown on over my pyjamas, and we headed out to the barn together. Mrs. Ewe was indeed in a state. We'd taken hot water with us, so Jim did the sleeves-rolled-up bit. Our worst fears were confirmed. She had been carrying not two, but three lambs!

This one had been dead for several days. It slithered out relatively easily, although one foot came off with the first attempt at pulling. The smell was so indescribably awful. Poor Mrs. Ewe looked dreadful, and we chose to support her one lamb with some bottle feeds for a day or two. Jimmy was beside himself that his former sleeves-rolled-up check after lamb number two had deceived him. He'd believed her uterus was empty at that point, and evidently it wasn't.

We laid the very smelly little body outside the barn doors before returning to Mrs. Ewe, getting her to take a few sips of water from a cupped hand. Fearful it would be some sort of scent-beacon for every carrion consumer in a three-mile radius, I declared I would remove the lamb and offer it to the pigs later that morning.

Our usual routine took over, and it was a few hours before I got back outside to give Mrs. Ewe another drink, give survivor lamb some bottle milk, and attempt to shovel up our casualty. Poor thing had frozen solid to the ground, and there was nothing I could do but leave it be.

By the time Jimmy got home again, the sun had been shining for just enough time to begin a thaw, and he prized the carcass up. While the pigs appeared to be equally appalled by the smell, I was not fooled in the least. I have witnessed pigs cheerily chow down on chicken guts and heads from our home poultry butchering. More likely, they were occupied with their grain ration, delivered just moments before.

Mrs. Ewe improved with earnest; every visit to her showed her in better and better condition. Even her lamb was feeding from her again. Her rear end was very swollen though. At first we worried about prolapse, but some communication with vets and a second opinion from our good neighbour led us to conclude it was really just swelling. A potent course of antibiotics to clear any residual contaminants and prevent infection was all it took.

It was maybe two weeks later that one of our remaining three ewes delivered her single lamb. She was a bit rubbish at cleaning him up, as in she didn't bother at all, but he was eager to get his first drink of milk and she was happy enough to stand for him. Jimmy took an old towel to the poor fellow, to dry him off and stop him shivering. We left the slightly neglectful mum and her baby to bond for a couple of days or so, before moving them into the same pen as our much-recovered Mrs. Ewe-of-the-Triplets. The first born of those triplets was still really small, and mum didn't seem to be producing much milk, although clearly enough to keep the wee fellow alive. Jimmy had nicknamed him Tippy, partly because the tips of his ears were an identical caramel brown colour, and partly because he was a triplet.

The two Mrs. Ewes did the usual power struggle and mad dash-about to establish who was who and which baby was which.

This season had been a big learning curve for me, as a complete novice to the lambing game. It seems ewes generally deliver their young and begin licking them in earnest right away to remove the amniotic-fluid-containing membrane, generally called 'the sac' in that delicate dialogue of Farmer-Speak. They also pretty quickly allow their tiny offspring to suckle, at which point the earnest licking becomes disturbingly concentrated on the baby's anus, as if to try and encourage that first poop that in human babies gets called meconium, and has the look and texture of road tar. I learned that this is how all Mrs. Ewes identify their own young – by a bit of bottom-sniffing.

When we mix them up a little, after a few days of cozy mum-and-baby time in their own jug, the ewes seem to go frantic trying to find the bottom that smells right. I have to wonder if there is a delightful smell to their own little darling's rear end, and no smell to anyone else's, or a non-smell for their genetic prodigy and an abhorrent stink to all others? Either way, it becomes a real three-ring-circus as ewes charge about the new pen sniffing every bottom they can find and choosing either to attempt protection in a poorly executed stay-beside-me-while-I-race-around-again or to head-butt the poor little critter into next week. The repeated chasing, sniffing, and bunting appears to create an ongoing picture of madness and mayhem designed to only further confuse unfortunate lambs caught in the middle of it all.

By the end of the day, we worried about little Tippy, as he seemed determined to try and access the overly-large udder and very in-your-face teets of Mrs. Ewe-of-the-Single-Lamb. I can't say that I blame him. Here was the Dolly Parton of sheep compared to his poor traumatized mum who had little if anything to offer with any regularity.

The racing around, bleating, and bunting continued with Tippy's resolve to gorge on that udderish bounty completely undiminished. We watched him hedge cautiously towards her when she was eating grain from the food bowl, sneak alongside her when her own lamb was feeding, and nip in quick as a flash for a single slurp when she was looking the other way. His persistence and determination were valiant!

By the next morning, Mrs. Ewe-of-the-Single-Lamb appeared to have accepted her fate in the rearing of two babies from her copious udder supply, with only an occasional side kick or evasive maneuver being employed. Even more amusing was what I can only describe as a matronly look of approval on Mrs. Ewe-of-the-Triplets face, each time Tippy scored another hit. Tippy's dogmatic enthusiasm put him somewhere between heroic warrior and artful dodger.

Having returned ewes and lambs to the corral, I pondered whether Tippy would feel like he was at the circus, dodging and feinting his way between all those Mrs. Ewes and their lovely udders, or whether he'd feel like he was in a never-ending boxing match, as each Mrs. Ewe bunted him seven ways from Sunday.

We had two ewes left in the barn, so far lambless. Jimmy thought we should get a look at their udders to see if there might be some promise of an imminent delivery or not. They were particularly skittish and it was a total sheep-rodeo to corner first one, then the other, to 'cop a feel' as one might say.

There wasn't much evidence of anything, but one ewe had a blue mark on her rump which indicated the ram had done what he's best at.

Here's how it works as far as I understand it: Ewes have a cycle (like all mammals) when they are sexually mature. It seems to be called 'estrus' with animals or sometimes 'in-heat'. Then, a male of the species is brought into the picture to encourage that whole procreation and reproduction thing. A lot of sheep farmers have big flocks or many flocks, and in order to keep track, the ram wears a crayon on his chest when he's let loose to do his Wild Thing with all those receptive ewes.

Don't think 'crayon' like a small child alternating between scribbling on freshly painted walls and swallowing unhealthy quantities of coloured wax. (My own eldest son performed his first art installation with crayons at the tender age of two. Unbeknownst to me, he had carefully placed a large number of coloured wax crayons into our old fashioned gas fireplace at our home in northern England during the summer. It wasn't until winter rolled around when we turned the gas fire on for the first time in months that "Voila!" his art was revealed. It ran all across the floor in what could have been construed by some as an impressive rainbow, but was construed by his mother to be firstly, the demise of our gas fire; secondly, a potential health risk; and thirdly, a major clean-up operation which she definitely did not need with two toddlers and a baby to contend with!)

No, this crayon is some kind of chalk-like block that gets fastened into a harness that the ram wears (think sheepy bondage gear) so that each time he mounts a ewe, the crayon leaves a mark. There are degrees of hardness and softness to these crayons, I guess to suit breed sizes, wooliness levels, or level of passion associated with doing the Wild Thing.

When Jimmy first saw the intensity of the blue on our ewe's rumps, he commented to our supplier that perhaps he could have used a firmer crayon. "Used the firmest" was the response. Our ram, named Neddy after the last ram in England Jimmy had, is an ardent and passionate lover.

So, there's one ewe with a blue behind, and another with no mark to see. Neither seem to be doing much other than eating grain and having a nice lie down.

Neddy is a character. I think I like him. When Jimmy and I walk up to the sheep corral, all our sheep go batty at the idea of forthcoming food. They huddle around the gate bleating like mad fools, not allowing us to get in. Their bleating never ceases to make me smile, as they always sound like someone doing the worst impression imaginable of a sheep, not really a "bah", but more the frantic yelps of a madman with a serious speech impediment.

We have perfected a system where I squeeze myself in first, with my bucket of grain held high enough that they can't stuff their heads into it and knock me over. Then, I slowly work my way through the frenzied crowd towards the nearest food trough, which under any other circumstances, such as when my tiny toddler grandson would like to pet and stroke a lamb, would cause them to run away in sheer terror before we ever got near them. I've little chance of pouring any grain into the trough, because of the crazy hullabaloo darting around in front of me. In the meantime Jimmy brings up the rear, with his two full buckets, plops one precariously on top of the large, round hay bale that lies within a gated feeder, and pours the other into the furthest trough.

The sheep never seem to understand the need to pour their feed out first, and diligently hamper our progress throughout. But Neddy seems to have figured out our system. He'll wait for the mad sheep crowd to move towards Jimmy; then, he'll go around to the far side of that first trough, look me in the eye, and patiently wait for me to start pouring from my bucket, pretty much right under his nose. He gets to tuck right into his breakfast while his many wives and offspring bounce back and forth between Jimmy and I, jostling to find a spot, only to decide on a better spot three seconds later. Amidst the mayhem, Jimmy will retrieve the bucket he left on the hay bale and pour that into the remaining empty trough.

Our lambs, a pretty hefty size by this time, still think they should stand in the food trough to eat the grain, a trick they employed when they were too tiny to reach in from the ground. But their large and cumbersome bodies now clamber and skid along in the trough, sending grain flying all over the place.

I have wondered about putting a pictorial poster in the corral that would describe step-by-step sheep etiquette, encouraging each ewe to find a place at the feed trough and stay there, each lamb to remain firmly connected to the ground, and everyone to eat only their fair share of breakfast at a pace that would be less likely to result in the hurling and spraying of food and potentially induced raging indigestion, than the galloping gluttony and frenzied feeding that normally occurs. But I know I'd be wasting my time.

***

Pasture time was becoming quite critical. We had used up the last of our hay bales, and the sheep desperately needed to be on some of that lush, green grass that was just colouring up nicely as Spring really picked up the pace. Jimmy had the brilliant idea of using our trusty electric chicken netting. It is quite the most versatile and fabulous device. We've used it very successfully on chickens before, and even on our pigs for six months or so as they 'piggivated' our first garden patch over the previous winter.

The netting is white, so very visible. It has horizontal electric wire alternating with a non-electric wire running the entire length. It consists of about ten panels, each beginning with a post that can easily be secured to the ground with two attached ground spikes, stretching almost two hundred linear feet. We have two, and they connect together to make any shape a person can think of to contain your critter of choice.

This time we were choosing sheep. Unfortunately, with almost thirty grown sheep and over thirty now-quite-large lambs, even our impressive netting enclosure was not big enough to provide an adequate grass area for our flock for more than about two days. The work of moving the netting every two days grew old very quickly!

A trip to Bulyea, a delightful small town about half an hour from us, gave us the bounty of fencing supplies we required,

including wire rolls and posts. Our budget couldn't stretch
to such purchases of course, but this has never stopped us
before; and, it wasn't going to stop us now. We've a tenuous
grasp on business principles, and prefer to just dive in and do
what needs doing. Our philosophy is that either it will all pay
off eventually, or we'll die one day and none of it will matter.

The important thing was to get those sheep a bigger area
of grass. Although we were still using the electric chicken
netting and moving it around every so often, we built our first
stretch of permanent fencing that would become a part of our
'map' of divided field areas, allowing distinct segments of our
farm for grazing, hay crop, and field grains and seeds for food.

Jimmy is a numbers person. He has admitted more than once
that he can't help himself. His brain begins counting at every
and any opportunity. He counts our lambs daily. This is no
mean feat. In the words of the lovely neighbours we bought
our flock from, they are "spry little gaffers", and run around
like components of a pinball machine without pause. To
count them is to take a series of mental snap-shots as they
bolt to-and-fro, and hope the numbers add up at the end.
Jimmy will count and re-count until he suspects he is in the
vague region of numbered correctness.

Later one evening, I had come home from a community
meeting with fellow members of the Lumsden and District
Arts Council, chauffeured by our licensed son, so that I could
take a bottle of wine with me to enjoy and share. I knew
Jimmy would be in the field working on the new fence for
the sheep, but it was quite a surprise to be greeted by him and
one of our younger daughters flagging us down and shouting

that there was a dead lamb to be dealt with. He quickly elaborated that it was stuck in the fence. Naturally, I thought it had somehow got tangled in the new three-strand electric fence Jimmy had been working on. The white chicken-netting has holes that are far too small to get a lamb's head through.

We headed up the field to learn more. It was the most unusual scene that greeted us. The south end of our corral had been fenced the previous autumn with an eight-foot-high page-wire fence (or pig-netting as I would have called it in England). It was our best effort to keep the coyotes away from our sheepy charges.

This type of fence has squares that are about four inches across, and our young lamb was wedged firmly into the fence. She had somehow not only pushed her head right out through one of the four-inch spaces, but she had also managed to turn her head back and thread it inwards through the next four-inch space in the fence, consequently garroting herself. At three months grown, this was quite a loss. Poor girl, she was Second Twin – the surviving twin from the early-departed First Born twin – the one who couldn't stand up despite having over-sized legs.

A more immediate worry than the untimely death of this lamb was the smell. Jimmy's counting, or more accurately counting-and-recounting-and-slightly-guessing, had not worked to identify the missing youngster right away. Tucked into that fence, hidden behind half-sized wood panels that form a sort of buffer zone between the high, wire fence and the paddock that only the smaller-bodied lambs can access, she'd been there more than a day. She was showing signs of bloat so pronounced that the upper side of her abdomen had already split open and was a hive of activity for blow flies and other passing insects in search of a quick feast. Our accompanying children scurried away with t-shirts held over their noses, uttering not-so-quiet protestations about being in the vicinity.

Jimmy had to cut the wire of the fence to release the head. I pulled the stinking corpse underneath the fence afterwards, as Jimmy held the lowest edge of the fencing up slightly with his foot. We didn't want to drag her through the paddock. Even when carefully pulling her by the back legs through the field area outside of the paddock, I was fearful of spilling her intestines out and creating a scent-beacon for those many beasties of the night.

We managed to get her onto the dropped tailgate of the truck, and drove the slowest and smoothest way home we possibly could. Even Big Butcher was not going to assist the piggies in access to this banquet; they were on their own!

We opened the fence a little, not willing to try swinging her over the top and covering ourselves in something unspeakable. We dropped her rather unceremoniously on the other side of the low electric wire that circuits the whole inside perimeter of the pig's run.

Pigs never seem phased by smells that would knock us humans sideways. In they went, straight for some decidedly gamey internal organs.

The day for shearing came along next. We'd had a blast of hot weather and felt genuine pity for some of our flock as they huddled in the shade inside their paddock. The crazy weather patterns of the year had brought us an ice storm only a couple of weeks before that though, so who knew when the 'right time' to shear was.

We contacted our friends, the suppliers of our sheep, to see when they were using a shearing crew so that we could hopefully persuade them to come our way. We were two weeks too late. Their crew had already come and gone. Jimmy did some hunting, and found a marvelous young lady from the next province who was willing to come to us in early June and undertake the work. An absolutely delightful father-and-daughter team arrived mid-morning, and Jimmy was immediately smitten by their very apparent Welsh accent, a sentimental reminder of our British roots.

The shearing began in earnest, and I was genuinely impressed with this young lady's skill. She had a fool-proof system for snagging one ewe after another. She used a hastily cobbled together race (single-file walkway) from our own on-hand materials and two custom-built holding pens. Each holding pen was just the size of a sheep that captured a "decoy" ewe to sit in the front pen for the duration of the job. Then, a steady stream of followers got tipped out of the second pen sideways, only to land squarely on their rump right between her feet. Genius! She also had an enduring sense of humour, even through the more challenging moments of mechanical breakdown.

With work underway, I had expected a sombre, focused atmosphere to descend upon us, and even anticipated a little grumpy, impatient attitude from time to time based on my ineptness at managing anything remotely close to useful... other than (badly) wrapping fleece and cramming it into the oversized hessian bag that hung high on a frame behind the shearing action. But no, our girl would raise her head from her intense sweat-producing work, smile, laugh and even add a little tidbit or anecdote to the ongoing conversations between her dad and Jimmy, who reminisced endlessly about all-things-sheep whilst driving one animal after another into the race.

We had deliberately procrastinated catching Neddy, even though he was such a docile chappy. When his turn came up, he was surprisingly obliging, and I wondered why I had been so worried. Our gal began her shearing pattern and made short work of his body fleece. As he sat there at her feet and she worked towards his head, she noticed he had a bit of a problem. One of Ned's back teeth had worked its way right through the side of his face, leaving a small hole in his cheek which displayed the green staining of chewed grass. As she sheared the wool away, she revealed the anomaly.

Quite the debate about potential remedies ensued, and our ignorance persuaded us to defer to the wisdom of our more experienced shearing team. The solution would be to either extract the tooth, or chisel it down to something within the buccal cavity confines, allowing Neddy's face to restore itself to something less leaky.

Armed with a pair of side cutters and some pliers at the ready, we restrained poor Ned to try some rudimentary dentistry, chipping away at the tooth until it felt smoother and somewhat flatter. We then released him towards a waiting trailer rather than with the other already-sheared ewes, so that he could spend the next little while in the barn with what were the two lambless ewes, for procreation purposes, as well as allowing us to keep an eye on him and that tooth.

The two lambless ewes were now actually only one lambless ewe. The other had ever so quietly and discreetly popped out a lamb in the early hours one morning thus revoking her lambless status.

This little fellow was almost three months younger than his frolicking counterparts out on field pasture, which meant his mum wasn't likely to be cycling (as in the estrus thing – nothing to do with bicycles) any time soon, and enticing Ned. Conversely, the remaining lambless ewe was welcome to entice Neddy as much as she could muster! Being occupied with these two ladies and his late-arrival offspring meant Neddy wouldn't have the opportunity to be sniffing around all the other ewes whose lambs were now of an age that cycling would be a-plenty.

All was proceeding splendidly until we began to notice that Ned wasn't eating any of the grain ration we supplied our small barn-dwelling group. Electric fence had been set-up around the yard to allow this little band of sheep to mow the lawn, and we had observed all of them munching away on the green stuff. Ned had received shots of antibiotics and anti-inflammatories on the advice of our vet post-dentistry, and he seemed to be well other than having a reluctance to eat grain. But it was a concern, especially as I remembered how clever he had been at standing in just the right spot at the corral to get first dibs on the grain we took there. We began to watch him closely.

Before too long we could see that Neddy was losing weight. His eating had declined and there was no option other than to put an end to his suffering. A friend had introduced us to a local chap who would do on-farm slaughter, and it was wonderful to meet this fellow and engage his services for Ned. We thought we'd try some of the resulting six-year-old ram, and paid to have his flesh ground up into hamburger-style minced meat at our newly-acquainted butcher's facility.

I love the concept of on-farm slaughter. I truly believe it is a happier and healthier end for an animal, without the stress of being loaded-up, driven-off, and herded-into some strange and unknown place that smells of death. But Public Health seems not to share my view. If I want to sell any of our meat at Farmers' Market (and at this point in our farming career the Market is our best way forward to create a customer or clientele base), it had to be slaughtered and butchered at a licensed facility, not in our barn.

Since Neddy would only be for us, this rule didn't matter, and it was by the end of that same week that we received a box of ground ram packages. Dropping his work off, our new friend commented that I might want to go heavy on the seasoning with this meat, because it was pretty "strong".

Ram curry! That would be just the ticket! I had kept a few frozen bags of murderously hot curry sauce in our deep freeze for at least two years which I'd made from some Trinidad scorpion peppers I had grown during our time in Ontario. I set-to with two packages of ground ram-meat and a bag of lava-like curry in the slow cooker for an overnight bubbling-and-simmering to tasty-up all that "strong" I'd been warned about.

I'd eaten mutton before and really liked it. Hosting an 'Open Farm' event back in Ontario, I had used ground mutton from a fellow Farmers' Market vendor to make mutton burgers, grilled on our own barbecue and sold to visiting 'Open Farm' enthusiasts, along with accompanying salads and sauces from other fellow vendors. It was so delicious that we sold out before the end of the day! But the early morning waft that greeted my nostrils from the slow-cooker after a night of cooking the curry was nothing short of revolting.It was sweaty-gym-socks revolting... intense-testosterone-laden-sheepy revolting.

I decided it wouldn't be fair to simply throw it all out without at least giving it a try. A person should never judge a book by its cover, or a flavour by its smell. There's a horrid stinky cheese that my dad once bought and ate (I think it was called 'Schaum's' maybe?) that smelled exactly like dog poop. I don't know how he got it past his nose and into his mouth, but he said it was great stuff. He had a similar story for that skanky fruit called durian. Who was I to sit in judgment of this foul-smelling stew?

I served a (very) small bowl, and took a (very) small teaspoon, not a teaspoon-full though, more towards the molecular end of the spectrum... just a tiny wee taste... and spat it out immediately! No, this was one of those times where it tasted exactly as awful as it smelled. Just for good measure, I got

Jimmy to try some too, and he concurred (probably whilst weighing up the pros and cons of becoming a single man again). The offensive offering found its way to the compost heap. I've no doubt the pigs would have tucked into Neddy with gay abandon, but I wasn't sure what those Trinidad scorpion peppers would do to the poor, unsuspecting squealers.

***

The last of the ewes were returned to the pasture, even our one lambless ewe who had earned the nickname 'greedy guts' from Jimmy, because she pestered and pestered whenever he was anywhere in the vicinity with a bucket.

Moving the electric chicken netting every couple of days became a regular chore, often done in the evenings. This led to a switch in our feeding time to supper rather than breakfast, to occupy the sheep ensconced in their corral while the fence was being moved. The growing appetite of the lambs was fast matching the appetites of their lactating mothers, and another trip to Bulyea for fencing supplies loomed.

Fencing is a necessary part of any livestock farming enterprise, and being new to this farm, with lofty ideas of rotational grazing and an adherence to biodynamic principles, we had hopes and dreams of segmenting up our land to give ourselves the best opportunity of achieving our goals. But fencing is a monotonous, repetitive, and thankless task.

I would summarise the whole process as: pound in a series of wooden posts, using a tractor-powered post-pounder, in our case borrowed from a very generous and helpful neighbour. Then, attach four foot perimeter page-wire fencing using five large and heavy staples, one on every other wire strand for each wooden post, hammered-in by hand (specifically Jimmy's hand. Menopausal hormones have put an end to any useful purpose my wrists may have had). Repeat. And, every now and then, when the roll of page-wire runs out (they are each over three hundred feet long), begin the new task of knitting together the ends of an old and a new roll into the pattern.

Monotonous, repetitive, laborious, and frankly never fully accomplished, I can see us fencing well into the next few years. Then, much like The Fourth Bridge, we will likely have to go back to the beginning and modify, maintain, and mend. A never-ending job.

***

We had missed adding the rubber ring to one of our lambs shortly after his birth in the spring. Not intentionally, we only noticed by chance one day, when we saw his dangly bits on display as he tucked into the grain that had been laid out in the trough for him.

As the time approached to butcher the first and largest group of lambs, Jimmy had the splendid idea of hanging onto this young chap, to replace his dad, Neddy. Of course, we would need to come up with a plan to separate him and the ewes from his half-siblings and his mum, but our optimism was nothing if not unwavering in the face of all challenges.

As the season drew to a close and we embraced the idea of making our next batch of lambs, I felt a surprising sense of accomplishment from our ambitious adventures. Roll on next season… when we will do it all again!

PART 2

Chicking

Whe bought an incubator and an automatic egg turner online. I had been investigating hatcheries for weeks. The pandemic of COVID-19 had somehow inspired the world and his wife to try their hand at hobby farming, and pretty much everywhere had sold out of day old chicks.

I wanted heritage breeds though, not the usual rake-thin, super-ovulating layers or can't-stand-up, super-fast growing meat birds. Not that I can criticize these breeds. They have served us well enough in the past. But with an eye on all things balanced, and in keeping with our organic and biodynamic practices, heritage seemed better.

I chose my hatchery, bearing geographical distance in mind, and selected as many eggs as would fill our egg turner: forty-one. A mix up in my original order and some communication with folks at the hatchery meant I ended up with forty-four eggs. We balanced the three extra over the top of the eggs neatly lined up in the turner, and we diligently turned those three by hand every morning and every evening, with the children taking turns and marking the deed on the calendar to prevent repetition.

Three weeks is quite a long time to wait patiently for eggs to hatch. The incubator instructions told me to fill the channels in the bottom with water, humidity being an important factor. The motor on the egg turner covered access to the sixth channel, but the other five were filled every morning. After eighteen days, the eggs get taken out of the turner and laid carefully on the floor of the incubator to be left alone for three more days until 'Hatch Day'. I made sure those channels were full of water with daily refills from a little plastic jug.

As complete novices to hatching eggs, we were astounded when we could hear cheeping before there was any sign of a chick or even a cracked shell. (We have since learned this is called pipping and is completely normal, but you can imagine our amazement back then!)

Our first chick hatched a day earlier than expected, and we stood hovering over that incubator like expectant parents.

The children named it and we watched with pure awe as it dried to a fluffy grey. I worried and fretted that it would get hungry or thirsty as the other chicks really took their time to make their breakthrough, but after two days, we had quite the crowd in that incubator. Chicks were staggering around like village drunks, crashing into eggs that were both part-way hatched or not yet hatched at all. That first hatchling surely was going to need some food or water soon!

It didn't take long before it was wet again. In fact, all the chicks were wet. The humidity levels were well over 90% and new hatchers were preventing it from getting any lower.

The air from the incubator vents smelled pretty bad and we could no longer see through the little perspex windows that were mounted in the lid, because there was so much condensation. I knew chicks that begin "gasping" are showing signs of dehydration, but I couldn't see through the windows to tell. A rising panic descended on all of us and we had several family conferences in the space of an hour or two to decide what our best option was.

We elected to open the incubator, remove all the wet chicks, and put them directly under a heat lamp in a prepared 'brooder' box that went behind the sofa in the living room of our home. Then, we would remove all the unhatched eggs into a bowl placing it also under the heat lamp in the brooder box. Next, we would wash out the whole incubator with hot soapy water and put all the part-hatched and unhatched eggs back in the incubator.

It turned out this was precisely what NOT to do.

By morning, ten of those wet chicks had died and were ceremoniously placed in the kitchen pig bucket. One part-hatched egg had also died. Two more eggs hatched, but only one managed to climb out; the other seemed to be stuck with membrane wrapped around its head.

After another rising panic sensation, I made another do-or-die decision. I reached into the incubator and unwrapped the little stuck chick leaving it in there to dry off with its friend. It was a very dark feathered blue Bresse, and much to my delighted surprise, it lived.

We left all the other eggs in the incubator for a couple more days, with high hopes of some more hatchlings delivering themselves into this world.

It was late morning when we heard the first "pop", not the pipping and shell-cracking indicative of new life that we were eagerly awaiting. No, the eggs were now EXPLODING inside the incubator! Even with our dash to turn off the heater and remove the eggs, placing them not-so-ceremoniously into the kitchen pig bucket, two more popped. The pig bucket was taken outside in a hurry, and delivered straight to the pigs who were absolutely delighted to be offered a side order of balut to their mainstay of pasture grass, grain, and kitchen scraps.

It took every ounce of self-control and grim determination to wash that incubator. The explosion had speckled every surface, including the heater and fan mechanism, with decomposed egg contents. I think I washed it at least three times, then disinfected it with hydrogen peroxide. Even then,

I had to leave it in direct sunlight for a few hours to eradicate the stink.

***

We are farmers and eternal optimists with an arguably questionable grasp on realism and the whole profit-and-loss concept. We don't let some trifling detail such as an 80% loss of hatching eggs deter us from trying again. I sat with one of my older daughters and we YouTubed ourselves into a stupor watching "How to Hatch Chicks" videos, taking notes on all the things we either did wrong or didn't do at all.

Our second batch of eggs arrived, not so many this time, just 30, and we followed all the advice to the letter. We rested the eggs for a day. I only filled one channel in the incubator with water, and monitored that humidity level like a thing possessed throughout the 18-day egg-turning period. At the beginning of our three-day "lockdown" period, I filled a second channel, but only halfway. It worked! By the time the first chick hatched, it raised the humidity level, but not so much that unhatched eggs would drown, and as the chick dried, the humidity level lowered, but not so much that hatching eggs would suffer shrink-wrapping from a dried membrane. We were able to observe through the little windows and even snatched out a fluffy dry chick or three, dropping in a wet paper towel or two to replace any lost humidity for the remaining hatchers.

This conjuring-magician-speed switch-out continued for a couple of days, snatching out dry chicks and replacing them with wet paper towel or snatching out wet paper towels when more hatching chicks knocked that humidity level way up there again. We were feeling pretty cocky about our successes.

The rate of pipping and shell-cracking indicative of new life slowed right down. Two active hatchers were tirelessly chipping away at their confines, but there was no sign of anything at all in the remaining eggs. Ever fearful of overdoing things and facing the horror of exploding eggs again, I was watching with bated breath. While one hatchling was free, running around and drying off, the other was taking an age to get out of its shell. For a whole 24 hours I kept checking on it. It was still alive, but seemed to be making no progress at all from the initial tear in its shell.

Well, young Blue Bresse from round one benefitted just fine from my assistance, and at this point, was outside in a lovely heated brooder pen in our barn, almost a month old and looking good. Perhaps I could be a hero for a second time, and just help this flailing little critter make some progress?

I had helping hands hold the lid of the incubator a bare few inches up from the base so that I could reach both my hands in and crack the egg open much as a person would do to make an omelette, but with rather different expectations. The chick was a wee yellow fellow, and it flopped out drawing big breaths onto the incubator floor. Membrane and shell seemed to be stuck to it in abundant quantities, so much so that I went in a second time to try and pick some off. So far so good! There were two little peepers running around in the incubator trying to dry off!

A day later (still extremely aware of the horror of exploding eggs), Yellow Fellow was still wet, and still very covered in shell. The children nicknamed him Shellybutt. We cast about for ideas and settled on using a hairdryer. After removing the other chick, now fully dry, into the heated brooder box with the others, I held the chick as gently as I possibly could, while moving the lowest and slowest hairdryer blower-setting across its whole body surface. It wasn't a wet feel though, but more a dried glue feel.

Try as I might, I couldn't change the nature of this chick's surface covering. My guess is the heroics just didn't cut it this time around. Forcing that hatch interrupted the natural timing of the process, and little Yellow Fellow had something like dried egg white stuck all over him. He didn't make it to the morning.

One of the successfully hatched chicks had a big problem going on. Almost immediately after hatching, while still in the incubator, we could see the chick just couldn't stand up. It looked as though its head was on the wrong way around. Every time it tried to stand or walk it fell over backwards and would wriggle and writhe on the incubator floor trying to right itself.

The other chicks (those not yet removed to the heated brooder box) took an alarming interest in this chick's exposed rear end while it wriggled and writhed on its back, and took to pecking at it. Dreading the carnage of them ultimately disembowelling the poor thing, we snatched it out of there with a prayer that it had dried off enough.

My older daughter consulted Dr. Google, and came up with

the diagnosis of 'wry neck' or the common term 'stargazer', because of the neck being twisted back to make the chick look as if it was gazing at the stars. Certainly genetic in this instance, it could have been a Vitamin E deficiency in the parent stock.

We began mixing milk and water to administer through a little dropper, and upgraded to finely-ground-chick-starter-porridge, also administered through a little dropper, every few hours. We even took ourselves off to the pharmacy to buy Vitamin E capsules and some selenium tablets (thought to help with the absorption of Vitamin E), and mixed those in with the porridge. Stargazer appeared to learn to open her beak during feeding times, and we were careful to go slowly and not gorge her with too much.

My younger daughter was most keen to be this chick's hero. Stargazer was kept in her own little box within the larger heated brooder box. She could hear her friends, but they wouldn't be able to peck her to death in their over-friendly way. Discussions were underway on how to move forward with Stargazer when it came time to transfer the fast-growing chicks out to the barn brooder with the much larger first nine.

Should she go with them and we make a rotation of feeding shifts in the barn? Should she remain in the house and we have an odd pet stinking up the place? In the end, it was a moot point. After 6 impressive days at surviving on her back pretty much the whole time, young Stargazer left this world to be in a better place where no one minds if your head's on backwards. My younger daughter was sad, but our many

Circle of Life talks allowed for a quiet acceptance and even an honouring of peace for the dearly departed chick.

All losses, oddities, and failed heroic rescues accounted for, we were at roughly a 50% success rate for our second batch of chicks. This was getting to be a really expensive group of birds, and it seemed time to address our questionable grasp of that pesky profit-and-loss concept, not least when my first survivor, that darkly feathered blue Bresse, turned its toes heavenward in the barn brooder. Dang that Circle of Life… I felt sad.

One of the other chicks from our first hatch, a Norwegian Jaerhorn, was showing some funny behaviours. It kept doing forward-rolls with its head twisted downwards and its toes all curled inward. We had been giving the chicks a multi-grain feed from a local organic farmer, along with regular, organic chick-starter. Perhaps the grains were knocking nutritional components out of balance? Maybe we should stick to only the chick starter ration?

We made our adjustments and added some hayseed (from the bottom of the wheelbarrow after Jimmy fed the cattle each morning). Mrs. Jaerhorn looked like she was showing some improvement. She could walk around without falling, and only occasionally looked like her head was on upside-down when she'd been curled up for a nap. I have experienced similar aesthetic disasters myself when first getting out of bed in the morning.

To address the profit/loss balance and still go ahead with our plans for the Most Fantastic Farm Ever, we ordered day-old regular brown laying hens from a not-heritage-at-all hatchery, and some day-old regular fast-growing meat birds. We added some day-old goslings to our order to make us feel happy and excited all over again! Jimmy grew up with geese on his childhood farm back in England, but this would be a first for the rest of us!

Our invoice arrived in the mail from the hatchery. They sent with it a Dos and Don'ts Idiot's Guide list of how to care for your chicks when they arrive. Right there in black and white were the words, "Do not add substances of your own choosing to the chick starter feed!" Ah.

We had noticed ongoing improvement with Mrs. Jaerhorn, who we were now not sure if she was actually a she, or even a Norwegian Jaerhorn for that matter. I may have confused the images I printed out to help us identify our birds, whose plumage seemed to be very non-conformist according to my expectations and the photos I'd printed. This bird may actually be a Swedish Flower. Nonetheless, the neck thing seemed to have righted itself once we fed the birds only chick starter, rather than our grand mix of seeds and grains, something apparently any idiot should have known.

I couldn't tell my Icelandics from my Blue Bresses, but I did very much enjoy simply watching my delightfully colourful brood each morning at feeding time.

We began work on a second brooder area in anticipation of the 96 hatchery birds due to arrive within two weeks. It needed to be a lot bigger than the current brooder, which only housed our 22 special super-expensive heritage birds.

Jimmy and I butchered a few rolls of mesh netting and cobbled together a critter-proof wooden frame to enclose the space. We had rigged a wonderful lifting mechanism to raise the front part of the mesh roof to allow us to get in and out without major contortionist manoeuvres.

It was 8:00am on Wednesday morning when I came back into the house to hear the phone ringing. With splash pants, winter gear, and rubber boots to remove before I could get to the phone, it was no surprise that it stopped ringing before I could answer it; however, my hasty shedding of outer layers meant I did get to see the caller identification still displayed on the screen: Canada Post. The missed call could mean only one thing – the chicks had arrived already!

Jimmy volunteered to high-tail it to the Post Office in town, and returned barely thirty minutes later with a large box of chicks and a small box of goslings. We hadn't even readied our water suppliers or our feeders. The Post Office doesn't officially open at that time in the morning! Foolishly we thought we had more time. The wonderful staff at our local P.O. did comment that they wouldn't have minded us showing up later to collect our boxes, as they enjoyed listening to the peeping and chirping that came from within.

The children came outside to join us, and we began to carefully pick out chicks, one at a time, and place them on the clean straw in their new home. We had a whopping four heat lamps shining above them.

The goslings seemed huge in comparison to the tiny brown and white chicks, but they were so soft and fluffy with outrageously huge webbed feet that we decided they were a winning favourite.

We lost the first chick the very next day. It's legs didn't work. It would dehydrate and starve if we left it, so it went straight to the pig pen. The day after, a second chick was cold and stiff on the straw, and met the same fate. By the end of the week, we noticed one of the goslings was looking a bit off, not keen to stand up, not quite opening her eyes and seeming very unsteady. We watched and waited for another day, but found her cold and stiff by the third morning. It seemed all the sadder, because one gosling lost from a total of six is a greater loss than two chicks out of ninety.

The second week went by and no one else chose to die. Jimmy and I took turns crawling into the low space we had made for them to refill with water and food. The lifting mechanism was excellent, but still left us with the tricky task of clambering right into a space that was only about three feet high.

The goslings chose to stay out of the direct heat from the heat lamp bulbs. They were often grouped together a foot or two away from the red glow. I was amused to no end to see them each morning with a chick or two wedged between them and even draped around their necks. One little brown layer chick was perched right on top of a gosling's back one morning, playing some feathered version of "King of the Castle'!

All of our children indulged in chick therapy, particularly during the online homeschooling weeks the pandemic enforced. Lunch times were less about eating, and more about cramming every second of the limited forty-five minute break into sitting with our fluffy babies, emerging with a Zen sense of universal calm and covered in chick poop, before tackling an afternoon of online classes.

The weeks rolled by and our goslings got so big that it didn't seem reasonable to keep them in the same space as the other little birds. In fact, we were beginning to think we had made a mistake putting the meat birds and laying hens together. The meat birds were greedy and always clamouring for food, diving in like things half-starved whenever we put the feed out for them. The little layer hens, just beginning to show their brown big-girl feathers, would leisurely stroll around waiting their turn for food that seemingly, they could happily take-or-leave.

First out were the goslings. We let them join the older super-expensive heritage flock that by now had the run of the whole barn. Jimmy did his best to keep them out of the stall that stored fresh hay for the cows, but they were singularly determined to access the big mound, and poop all over it.

The goslings spent all their time warning us and their fellow chickens of impending disaster; a constant 'weep-weep-weep' sound came from their collective group of five as they waddled their beautiful, round, Jemima-Puddleduck bottoms along.

The plumage on the heritage birds was a sight to behold! Three roosters had revealed themselves so far, with competitive cock-a-doodling whenever the fancy took them. My Swedish Flowers' were a beautiful speckled brown, with

Mr. Flower sporting an impressive display of punk-plumage in copper, black, and gold. Two Jearhorn roosters were a spotty black-and-white, with very large and very red combs and wattles. I had a gorgeous pale grey Mrs. Bresse, and more all-black Bresses from the second hatch, not yet telling us their gender.

It was the highlight of our feeding chores for me to just stand and watch our birds in the barn. The goslings liked to practice ballet, stretching a leg and a wing all the way out behind them in a slow and graceful movement before settling back into a lazy huddle in the much-coveted and totally-forbidden hay.

Tackling the mix of laying hens and meat birds was a different challenge, mostly because we weren't dealing with only five big birds! We pondered the merits of leading the greedy meat birds out with the promise of food, but imagined a less-than-successful outcome involving a mad scramble of demented poultry racing around the whole barn, devouring grain assigned to older birds and pooping (heaven forbid) all over the fresh hay stall. I had suggested we construct a dividing wall of netting down the middle of the existing area, but we ruled it out on the basis of not wanting to work a construction project whilst bent double like a pair of old crones in the three-foot-high space.

Jimmy climbed in (bent double like an old crone) and passed birds out to me, two-at-a-time when he could, for me to carry to the next stall that we had chick-proofed with a bit of mesh netting here and there. We learned two things from this exercise. The first was that the decision to not work in bent-double conditions was the right one (at least for me). Jimmy was sweating and stiff when he finally came out of there. The second was that we had not adequately chick-proofed the next stall with our bits of mesh netting.

We didn't discover the latter bit of information until the next morning when the ever-hungry meat birds saw us carrying pails of grain for them. They broke out of their warm and cozy home to run around in a state of perpetual panic, trying equally hard, but with less success to get back into their warm and cozy home when they saw where the grain was heading to. Of all our calamities, this one was an easier fix than most, with only the need of a few minutes with a staple gun to make everything right again. Even catching the escaped chicks wasn't so bad. One consequence of their voracious appetites is a slight disadvantage in the running-away department.

Feeding the laying hens by themselves was a stark contrast. Jimmy did a high-pitched voice-over of our ladies politely procrastinating over their breakfast... "No no, you go first Daphne. I'm really not all that hungry. No no no, honestly Maude, I absolutely insist you take a bite before I do... I'm counting my calories you see." I was laughing so hard I almost peed my pants.

We took the decision to let our bigger birds have a taste of the great outdoors, and wedged the barn door open for them to come and go as they pleased. They did not venture far in the early days, scuttling back into the barn for safety if the wind blew or a pig barked. (I do mean 'bark' rather than grunt... They grunt a lot, like a low-level chatter between themselves, but in any foray for food scraps, or a skirmish over pot-holes or mud-baths, they will bark like a dog at each other.)

Pretty soon the goslings, in particular, became intrepid adventurers. Noted for their ability to forage, they preferred to consume large quantities of our wild grasses, which we deliberately and rather lazily allow to grow long.

The idea of 'wilderness patches' came from a visit to an organic seed company on Wolf Island in Ontario some years ago when we lived out there. By only mowing pathways in a lawn to allow unimpeded access to designated areas, the remaining grass and all other vegetative life-forms can be left to do their own thing, giving rise to some surprises gifted by Mother Nature as well as a small sanctuary for passing or inhabiting wildlife. It is also a veritable haven for insects.

It seemed to be a gosling's paradise! At least, until it wasn't. Whether she got under a cow's foot, or whether she collapsed for no good reason at all, we found one of our beloved five dead in the cow pasture right next to the barn. She was fairly squished, but with no other sign of predator injury. We leaned towards hoof damage as the cause without any other explanation for her deflated look on hand. Poor thing.

Now we were down to just four. I had a stern word with them about looking out for themselves, but waggling those beautiful, big bottoms was all they offered me in return. With an abundance of feathers being a bigger challenge than wool for pigs to consume, we buried young Jemima in the compost heap.

The heat increased. The rains came and the grass grew even longer. Nothing entertained me more than watching our goslings with their big, waggly bottoms, stretching their necks forward until they were nearly horizontal and "mweep-mweep-mweeping" their way around the yard. Sometimes they would follow us back to the three-door shed after our feeding rounds in the morning, trotting along with their ungainly webbed feet and their wings spread wide. I couldn't decide if they were trying to warn us away in territorial goose-speak, or whether the gesture was "Wait up! We want to come with you!"

Our expensive heritage birdies were less adventurous, only taking a few steps outside the barn doors and then dashing back inside at any noise, movement, or bit of breeze. Mr. Flower seemed the bravest of our growing roosters, and earned himself the category of 'keep'.

It was becoming more obvious that most of our blue Bresses were roosters. I counted five if wattle and comb were anything to go by. Only the odd time could I catch one practicing his cock-a-doodle. This was okay though, the French breed is a delicious meat bird apparently, and since our regular cornish cross meat bird flock consists of mixed males and females for butchering, I could see no reason why a young Bresse male would be any different. 'Soup hens' or 'roosters' tend to mean laying birds no longer laying, or roosters who have been around for a while; tough old birds, but good for stock or soup making. I wanted to try one of our Bresse boys myself though, before waxing lyrical about their merits in public.

We were approaching the time where separating our birds into appropriate flocks was necessary. It would be no good breeding out those lovely meaty characteristics by letting

47

skinny layer breeds such as my Icelandic rooster do his Wild Thing with our buxom, busty girls. But, as often happened, events did not quite pan out the way we had hoped.

We had watched the young Bresses, most of whom were from the second hatch back in March, to determine if those five male suspects were indeed of the "boy" persuasion. One of our morning rounds of feeding our many critters, I noticed an increase in the cock-a-doodling of the Bresse boys, and a worrying amount of sparring, face-offs, and skirmishes between them and the other birds.

Two mornings later, I witnessed a full-on assault of the randy rooster kind on one of the older Swedish Flower hens. Poor love. She didn't know what had hit her, and remained crouched and trembling on the ground after we pushed off the adolescent lout. True compassion came in the form of one of the Norwegian Jaerhorn roosters, who stood next to poor Mrs. Flower and even gently preened some of her feathers in an effort that looked for all the world like a hug.

Plans changed that same day. Instead of trying to separate out the layer-hen-varieties of rooster, we quickly had to separate out the aggressive Bresses who showed no manners at all.

God bless the electric chicken netting, which had only recently had a reprieve from sheep fencing. An old, but quite large dog kennel that had been left on the property served to house our five delinquents inside the chicken netting. There were also three or four big old trees nearby to provide shade on the hot and sunny afternoons.

Within days we experienced the first 'break out' when Jimmy

caught a couple of cocky Bresse Boys nestling a nice dirt bath for themselves amongst my hollyhock seedlings. He snatched up both cheeky brutes and put them back in their run. The hollyhocks were seriously depleted in number, but my hope was high for the few survivors.

A few weeks later, I found one Bresse boy marching around my vegetable garden, playing "catch-me-if-you-can." I tried and failed to sneak up on him, succeeding only in pulling out a handful of tail feathers. In fairness, he was probably only being smart; I tend to favour dropping pulled weeds onto the ground, as I think of all the lovely nutrients the weed took in during its growing period that could then be returned to the soil for the plants growing there. Sometimes, though, I'll reserve a handful of lovely, long, seedy grasses or a bunch of flowering mustards, and throw them into the run for our boys to munch on.

I'll bet Billy Bresse watched me around the veggie garden pulling those weeds, and knew exactly where the tasty treats came from. "Have wings will fly." He thought he'd go and get his own! Eventually trying to force his way back into the run by poking his head through the netting and getting stuck, I was able to grab him and plunk him back over to the right side of the fence.

We had our ram, two ewes, and a lamb temporarily in the barn, occupying one of the end stalls overnight. Whether Mrs. Swedish Flower had tried unsuccessfully to evade an advancing sheep's rump as it plopped down for a rest, or whether she found herself on the receiving end of a particularly firm bunt, I'll never know. We found her cold and stiff at the edge of the stall, just as if she had been trying to squeeze under the rails dividing that stall from the next.

By the end of July, we were finding our first eggs. These would be from our girls surviving that very first hatch in February. I had folks at Farmers' Market asking me for eggs already, as I had been a bit premature in my advertising. I debated taking just that one first egg and placing it on my table saying "Egg! I have an egg!"

The separated Bresse Boys were still at-large in the temporary chicken-netting run at the start of August. One rooster was out-and-about running loose around the garden, as we walked a construction team around our yard in anticipation of some much-needed renovations to our house. Our youngest and myself made a half-hearted attempt to catch the bird and plunk him back where he belonged, but he was fast – too fast and too artful in his dodging – for us to succeed. Once our visitors departed, it took three of us to corner this feisty little fellow and return him to his quarters.

Our youngest child stood guard and watched for a while as I fetched the day's laundry to hang on our washing line. "They're picking on him" was the concern I heard when I returned with my loaded tub of wet washing. And indeed they were… the other four roosters were mercilessly charging after this poor fellow and trying to stab at his head and sides with their beaks. He would push his head through the netting while they crowed and pecked at him, then pull back, break into a run and try to escape their attack with a dodge, a feint, and a sprint to another area.

We watched this repeated behaviour for a minute or two,

while we talked about what could be done. Could we move our poor victim back to the barn? But we had just removed these boys from the barn. Plus there were four other roosters still in the barn with our forty-ish laying hens, and already I was having doubts about keeping even that many in there.

As we ruminated and observed, we were both taken by surprise as our young fellow pushed not just his head, but his whole body through the netting, and took a sigh of relief as he realised he had once again managed to evade his tormentors, slowing his pace to a calm stroll through the tall grass of our nearest wilderness patch. We employed the timeless solution to so many problems… "do nothing". He got his own little water dish, and we left him to roam about the yard in much the same way as our barn-residing birdies do. To him, the barn was as far as the next city, and he didn't find his way over there to try his luck with the ladies. Instead, he hung about the perimeter of the netting enclosure, unsure of whether he was in a better situation or not for being on the outside. Our youngest named him Gregory.

The geese began developing a 'honk'. Think of the average adolescent male and the squeaky-breaking-voice chapter that comes with puberty. It sounded like something between the "mweep" noise of the gosling and a bark, more or less a loud sneeze really.

We had learned that our geese definitely just love being around us. They'll chatter with excitement and rush to see whatever it is we're doing when we go out each morning.

Our eldest daughter had been a repeat visitor with her

fostered dog throughout July enough times that the geese recognised them both. If she took her dog out of our yard and onto the grid road for a walk, they'd chatter and flap and run after them. "Come back! Come back!" they'd cry. If we had company, they would sidle up with their heads tilted sideways, pointing that one beady eye to ask, "Who are you?"

Although it was later than we would have liked, we had managed to move our hulking meat birds outside and onto pasture, in early July. A chance purchase of a very sturdy three-sided shelter from a neighbour who no longer needed it, was the perfect solution to the conundrum of sheltering that had kept them confined to the barn for as long as it had. The structure was quite similar to the pig shelter Jimmy had built earlier in the year, but with a lower roof line. The wooden skids underneath not only stood being dragged across our field, but had held together when the neighbour dragged the shed to us along typically rough Saskatchewan grid roads from more than two miles away.

We modified its former use with bovines and equines to become more suited to poultry, adding a front of mesh that included a wooden-framed door we could secure closed at night. Without a floor, the ground beneath the shelter would benefit from all that pee and poop. We moved it over a full length every few days so that the birdies' bottoms stayed clean, and a fresh piece of pasture was available outside of the shelter by correspondingly moving the electric chicken netting, which surrounded the opened pen throughout the day.

It took a few days for our birds to understand that grass and bugs were edible and plentiful; initially they still fixated on anyone carrying a bucket and were relentless in their endeavours to get underfoot and trip a person right over.

With their age and their size, meat birds can often become a little cannibalistic and start pecking at each other. This short period of transition to pasture resulted in one such casualty – a smaller hen whose wing-joint had been half-eaten when we went to them for our morning chores. The problem is that apparently chickens (who are virtually unchanged from the dinosaur version of themselves I learned!) will zone-in on the sight of flesh. What might have been a minor injury to begin with will be incessantly pecked at and exacerbated, until it is an ugly open wound, which, of course, invites further zoning-in and pecking.

I dashed off to fetch some cloth, iodine, and some umbilical binding tape that had been left by former occupants in our barn. We sprayed wingless-henny-penny with the iodine, placed one clean cloth between her body and the underside of her wing, and another over the top of her wing, and bound around her whole torso with the tape. She was startled and a little traumatised by our ministrations, and just sat perfectly still when we returned her to the fenced run. The cloth served to prevent any further beaky interest in her shoulder joint, but when the poor soul felt brave enough to try joining her savage flock-mates and stand up, the binding tape served to keep her permanently off-balance. She tilted and lolloped, ultimately falling into a heap, which dislodged the binding tape so that it both tripped her up and loosened the top clean cloth, exposing her injury, and instantaneously exciting her flock-mates into a frenzy of chasing, zoning-in, and pecking.

Jimmy fetched his axe as I gently carried our casualty back to the yard. I set a pan of water to boil in the kitchen on the stove, and we set to hand-plucking (no sense in setting up the electric plucker for just one bird). We ate barbecued chicken for supper.

Once those few transitional days passed, our meaty birdies morphed into totally different personalities. There was no more cannibalism for one, regular and careful inspection every morning revealed not a jot of blood or missing feathers on anyone. They would still go nutty at the sight of a bucket, of course, and Jimmy developed some very clever tactics to prevent accidental death by being trodden-on.

Evening bedtimes involved taking the chickens their grain for supper, enticing them to go back into the predator-proof shelter for the night. To stop them from getting right under his feet in their excitement, Jimmy would walk to the far side of their run once he was inside the electric netting, where they would follow him like he was the pied piper. He, then, would break into a sprint to get to the shelter ahead of them (not hard when we compare Jimmy's super-long stride with our fat birdies' barely-balanced waddles on their little chicken legs), pour grain in a long line down the middle of the shelter, allow plenty of space for all the birds to line-up and share when they finally got there, and lock the door behind him to keep them safely contained for the night.

The morning routine was water-replenishment only, but the water was still delivered *in a bucket*. In this case, the birds were all still locked-in from overnight, but the large water dispenser was of course locked-in there with them.

Having set it close to the door though, it wasn't too difficult to reach in, while barring the way out for eagle-eyed bucket seekers, snatch up the waterer and hold the door shut to keep escapees contained, while the ritual of emptying remaining water out, rinsing the container parts, and re-filling with fresh water was completed. When the empty water buckets were safely removed from view outside of the chicken netting fence, our charges could be released.

The once almost savage and wild behaviours of these birds were now replaced by a calm and serene devotion to the ground underfoot. Our chickens would exit their shelter without screeching, fighting, or clambering over one another, just quietly and slowly hop over the door sill, two or three at a time, and venture out to explore what new delights the grass and soil would yield for consumption that day. Right away the flock would fan-out in the available space, dedicating intense interest in nearby grass blades or seeds, or peck into the soil to grub out some small critter.

Gregory continued to hang-out right beside the netting that contained his brothers. He looked incredibly keen to be back in there with them. They looked like they were missing him too, sitting close to him on the other side of the fence. It was only a day or two later that one of the brothers, a very beautiful, meaty, blue-black creature, flew right over the top of the chicken netting, and had a nice trot around the grassy area surrounding their run. In the time it took Jimmy to relay what he had seen to me, and for the two of us to walk back over to that spot, he had returned himself to his run. The behaviour was repeated in the following few days. He'd fly out, and then back in, out, in, like a poultry hokey-pokey.

Another of the brothers, with dark-and-light-grey feathering like Gregory, learned the same trick. We wondered if there was any point in having the electric chicken netting up at all.

Feeling bold and brave in their numbers, Gregory and his grey brother would venture towards the barn every now and then, whether spurred on by the ceaseless cock-a-doodling that emanated from the structure, or suddenly catching sight of all those beautiful hens.

There were four roosters still with all our barn hens. Each of them had been given a name by the children: Ruffles was our Swedish Flower boy; Rocky and Salsa were the two Norwegian Jaerhorn brothers; and Jalapeno was the Icelandic rooster. Ruffles predominantly led the assault charges to keep the Bresse brothers at bay, with one or more of the other roosters acting as back-up. For the first day or two, Gregory and his cohort couldn't get past the small brow of ground up near our potting shed, because Ruffles and his sidekicks would come bounding up the slope with feathers plumped and an attitude for action. Greg and brother would retreat post haste, only to give it another try five minutes later.

Jim worried about Gregory being out by himself at night, although the first night he got shut into the barn. It was quite by accident; Jimmy just hadn't spotted him in there. The second night he saw Gregory hunkered down in the furthest corner of the barn away from all the other birds, but he sauntered out unperturbed first thing in the morning ready for another day of cat-and-mouse. It seemed our boys only got all territorial and boisterous in the daylight hours.

I felt for Gregory though. He never went back into the run with the other Bresses, just lurked around that area of our yard. He never had much success bonding with the barn birdies either, getting chased off all the time. I wondered if he felt lonely, or depressed even?

He had taken to watching me when I hung the laundry on the line (a daily occurrence through the summer months, with the large number of clothes-wearing people in our household). He would cock his head and keep one eye on me, much like the geese do sometimes. "Poor, sad Gregory, am I your only friend?"

"We should probably butcher them all soon," was my thought-of-the-day which I gave voice to when Jimmy came across to the washing line. Gregory's little water bowl became a toy for the geese, who would chase him off and try grabbing the edge of it to flip it over, spilling all the water. I replaced it with a bigger, rubber tub, which was less tippable, but also favoured by the geese, who had so far scored almost half a dozen water bowls around the yard, one of which was big enough to swim in.

We moved the mobile chicken shelter that housed our burly meat birds and its associated electric chicken netting every few days, to give them fresh pasture to graze on, and a clean house to sleep in. The first time we tried this we had hoped the birds ensconced within the shelter would just rumble along inside in time with the extremely slow speed of the tractor that pulled the shelter on its wooden skids. Each end of the shelter has a wooden "skirt" that we added to keep chickens in and predators out. We had naively thought this would suffice to 'brush' the chickens along.

We had barely progressed a couple of feet when two white bodies came tumbling out the back end. Mercifully, the gaps were large enough that they were unharmed, but it was a steep learning curve for us. Chickens don't understand that they need to keep pace with the unseen tractor. They will just allow themselves to be mowed down, confused and likely feeling very chicken-little-ish, with less of the sky-falling-down and more of the-floor-speeding-up feeling!

It was around the fourth time of us moving this shelter that I had my first moment of panic. I had perfected the dubious task of having myself locked into the shelter with the chickens, shooing them forwards, away from that back wall, and then walking along with them, slowly waving a long stick back-and-forth to keep them from venturing towards that back wall and being dragged underneath it. Health and Safety would have had a hissy fit for sure!

Once or twice our youngest would come out with us on the shelter-moving days, and he would act as a relay-voice between mum locked-in the chicken shed and dad driving the noisy tractor that pulled us along. But on this occasion it was just me, imprisoned with our birds, and Jimmy up front, making it all happen, unable to hear anything at all. He had steered ever-so-slightly sideways, following a map in his head that formed a short arc in the traversing of our caravan. My stick-waving protective maneuvers were brilliant for straight-on linear progression, but were ill equipped to cope with the enormous deviation of a slight turn.

First one, then a second chicken went under the front-side wooden skid rail as the building lumbered forward. Even the glacial pace we were moving at was too fast for me to stop their legs getting rolled and seemingly mangled underneath the heavy wooden frame. They screeched and squawked, and I panicked. I used my stick to try to pry them loose, all the time fearing for the birds I was ignoring, and even for myself. I was worried that we could all end up being mowed down by the shed. They were stuck fast, and being dragged along. It was awful. I could see us having chicken on the barbecue for supper again… if I lived to see supper again.

Time seemed to stretch, the way it does when something awful happens. It was really just seconds, but somehow time yawns into slow-motion while the awful thing is actually happening. Then, suddenly the birds were free, just like that! They wobbled and were obviously flustered, but they joined the rest of the crowd. My stick-waving returned to its former glory, as if nothing had happened at all, and the tractor slowed to a stop, all in less than five seconds.

The whole moving exercise was probably ten seconds at most. Jimmy came to the door to let me out, and could see that disaster/panic/trauma was written all over my face. "Are you alright?" he asked, "You didn't shout, did you?"

No, I hadn't called out to him. I doubt it would have done any good if I had. Imagine trying to extricate two stuck chickens from underneath a stationary building? At least while on-the-move, my prying and poking had a chance of working, and it did.

We opened the door once the electric chicken netting was re-established to give them a new bit of pasture to peck and forage in. We watched carefully as each bird emerged to spot any injured parties. There was a minor abrasion on one of the birds, with a small amount of blood, and she seemed oblivious to her damage, not even limping, but the last bird to emerge from the shelter hobbled quite a bit. Jimmy lifted him up and we thought he'd ripped out a fair amount of chest and tummy flesh with the amount of blood on his underside, but no. Closer inspection revealed that it was just his foot, badly skinned, and looking quite swollen. It had transferred blood to his white belly feathers. I ran for the iodine as Jimmy cradled our casualty. We doused both birds, and stood to watch for a while.

When Sir Limp-a-Lot stood up, another bird would zone-in on the sight of blood and try to peck at his foot. Jimmy commented how interesting it was that these birds, and most creatures if we're being honest, will seek out the weak, sick, or injured, and annihilate them right away. Humans do quite the opposite. We nurture our sick and injured, giving oodles of time, money, resources, and effort to helping them rejoin the pack. Not right; not wrong. Just interesting.

We decided to keep an eye on him, as he learned right there and then that if he just sat down, no one could see his bloody foot, and they left him alone. He was fine, and two days later wasn't even limping. We couldn't spot him any more in the crowd of bumbling, hulky meat birds.

I did take the time, in the small hours before dawn, (as is often the best time for such things), to problem solve a less tight-rope-walking experience for future shelter-moving days.

The next two moving occasions involved letting the birds out beforehand. This was much easier as they would wander around nibbling at grass, allowing us to slide the shelter forward. The difficulty came when we took down the electric chicken fence, and they had the opportunity to saunter all over the field. But it was a manageable task to corral them back into the designated area, as they are not blessed with speed.

We had spent a long time trying to address the problem of butchering chickens. Historically, we have always slaughtered and butchered for ourselves, but Public Health doesn't like this approach if we intend to sell commercially, like at our Farmers' Market stall. Nowhere could we find a licensed premises willing to oblige us, not without obscene driving distances that would both stress the birds in transit and stress the credit card with fuel bills.

With a sigh, we pulled the plucker from the dark recesses of the shed, sharpened the axe, set water to heat, and processed twenty birds, including the naughty Blue Bresses. I had high hopes of those Bresses, having read up on them at the hatching egg stage. But right at the point of dressing (an odd term for ripping the guts out of a bird, when it suggests something more towards putting clothing on), I could tell that "succulent", "juicy", and "tender" were complete misnomers. There was little enough meat observable on them post-plucking. Also, when forcing my hand into the body cavity, as is necessary to scoop out the contents, the membranes, and interstitial tissues, they would not rip easily. The phrase "tough as old boots" sprang to mind.

Still, ever the optimist, I reserved two carcasses for supper the next night. Perhaps I was being unfair comparing them to regular, plump meat birds. Perhaps the flavour of the lesser quantity of meat would be superior.

A stint in the oven, roasted with carefully selected and prepared veggies from our garden proved my suspicions true. We couldn't even eat the legs. Chicken pot pie after some serious stewing for a second go-around was enough to shatter all my romantic illusions about this heritage bird being a fine centre-piece for the table.

The remainder of our meat flock were destined for home-butchering too, although we hoped to employ a friend we had made earlier that year who took care of the slaughter of our ram. He had the delicate butchering skills that Jimmy and I lacked, and our goal was for portioned cuts of chicken, not just whole roasting birds.

Our egg layers were doing a fine job, with more and more hens adding to the supply of eggs each morning. When I took eggs to the Market, I sold out within the first hour!

All in all, I felt our journey along the Poultry Path had been quite the adventure, from those early hatching eggs and day-old babies, to the proud flock of chickens and geese that graced our farm yard. It was good to be a supplier of organic meat and organic eggs to the folks for whom these things matter.

PART 3

Cowing

Jimmy grew up on a dairy farm, and he loves cows. I thought I might love cows too. I would frequently go out into the fields with Jimmy when we were first dating. Completely new to this farming lark, I thought I could just don a pair of wellies and it would all come naturally to me.

Then, I met Mr. Hereford. He was a steer (I had yet to learn the intricacies of Farmer Speak, never mind the complicated terminology of what sort of cow a person was dealing with), which means a boy cow minus his procreating boy-parts, or testicles, to use more familiar biology-speak. Until this point in my life, steer was something I thought you did with a car, or maybe a bike. To this day, I remain ignorant of what it was exactly that inspired some historical farmer person to choose the word assigned to intentional-vehicular-direction-choice to describe a boy cow without his dangly bits. I suspect Mr. Hereford was equally ignorant, because he didn't seem to comply with the prescribed behaviours of a non-testosterone male. No, Mr. Hereford thought he was a bull, or at least that was what I believed.

I would be the all-helpful-girlfriend-on-the-farm when Jimmy wanted to take a bale of hay into the field, and walk alongside the skid steer (see, there's the word steer again, only in the context of skidding now) while Jimmy was driving. This is when Mr. Hereford would spot me and my very obvious aura of sheer terror, and think it would be an absolute wheeze to charge right at me. The more I dodged and ran around the little machine Jimmy was safely encapsulated in, the more Mr. Hereford rose to the challenge of scarring me for life by playing the role of some beast-like overgrown puppy wanting to play. Jimmy even said, "He's only being playful," which I thought was fine banter from a man sitting inside a motorized cage while his betrothed ran for her life and screamed hysterically.

Interestingly, I went ahead and married Jimmy anyway, and some time later that same year I took great satisfaction in chowing down on a Mr. Hereford steak. Karma.

We immigrated to Canada with a two year old child and a six month old child, after only four years of marriage. The call of farming was much more answerable on Canadian soil, after those four years had been spent fruitlessly trying to secure even a tenancy on an antiquated feudal-system-style farm in England.

Adventure is my middle name, and the allure and excitement of a new chapter in our lives that involved a whole other continent was too strong to resist. We had actually never even heard of Saskatchewan until we met up with an agent willing and able to connect the dots for us, and send us farm-hunting in the province that we would eventually call home.

After almost eight years of conventional grain farming, we changed our focus. It had been a while since Jimmy had worked with cows… and it was time.

Maggie and May were Holstein/Ayreshire, lovely old bony coat-rack black-and-white ladies, that we bought already in calf. Here, I must comment on the Farmer Speak again. "In calf", which sounds rather macabre and worrisome, actually means the reverse of a literal interpretation. The calf was, in fact, inside the cow. Biology-speak would call this pregnant. Anyway, it wasn't long before the calf was outside of the cow (a process I learned was called "calving", not to be confused with "carving" which would invoke equally macabre and worrisome images), and our lovely, gentle, and generous cow shared her milk with both her offspring and us.

They were lovely and gentle, but when I mentioned I was scarred for life by Mr. Hereford, I wasn't exaggerating. I could no more go into that cow field than I could fly to the moon. I tried to remedy this with horses. Our older daughters had joined us on Canadian soil by this time, and were eager to do the horsey thing. We found a wonderful local establishment that catered to such things, and before you could say "saddle", we had bought two mares as riding horses.

Whilst our daughters attended riding lessons and took the four-leggeds out for a trot, I braved-up and took to brushing and grooming these giants. They would stand perfectly still and let me brush their coats. I even built enough courage to have a go at hoof-picking. "Well how hard can it be?" I thought to myself, watching one of my daughters gallop along the dirt track.

My history of riding lessons is so short it will barely make a sentence; however, I did expand my horizons to encompass driving horses. Definitely not the same as "steer". To drive a horse is to either walk behind it or sit on a piece of equipment behind it that the horse pulls along. I was so determined to pursue this new avenue that I sought out old fashioned horse-drawn farm equipment, and spent a sizeable sum on collecting it.

I paid for two beautiful Clydesdale draft horses that I hoped to work with and build my dream farm; a throwback from Victorian times with horseshoes and plough-shares my mainstay. But, Mr. Hereford had made more of an impact than I had given him credit for. It was no use. Despite my keen efforts and some of the best coaching imaginable from a dear friend and neighbour who had raised, owned, and continued to house my Clydesdales, I could not shake my innate fear of animals bigger than me.

Our older daughters eventually moved on with their lives, to university and gainful employment. The riding horses also moved on, sold to a better and more involved family, and my Clydesdales never even left the farm on which they had been born and raised. The antique farm machinery got passed along too. When the books say, "If you want the dream of a horse-drawn hay cart, buy a Constable painting," they aren't wrong.

***

Maggie and May were Jimmy's territory, not mine. In order to get them in calf again, we borrowed a neighbour's highland bull. He was just about the funniest little guy to look at; one of his horns pointed upwards, the other downwards. His fur was long and bright orange, and he was very short. I looked at him and looked at Maggie and May, and I told Jimmy we would need to get an orange crate for him to stand on.

I think that phrase "orange crate" comes from some old English mentality, when oranges actually came from afar in wooden crates that you could then use to stand on and reach for things on the top shelf. If your partner was much taller, you would joke that you needed an orange crate to be able to kiss him. In Highland Bull's case, I figured he would need an orange crate to do the deed we needed him to do with Maggie and May.

Then, one morning Jim came in from the field with a grin and said, "He doesn't need an orange crate at all!" Leaving you with that mental image, I can say that he did his job very well and even though we sold Maggie and May before we left that farm, we learned they both had healthy calves. I've often wondered if they were orange or had wonky horns.

We left them behind to begin a new adventure in Ontario, and once we'd settled on our Ontario farm, we began looking for a new cow. Some friends shared a magazine for small farmers, and I found an advertisement at the back for a Jersey cow. We contacted the owner and made arrangements for her to be transported to our farm.

She was a lovely thing. Her mum had died after she was born, and the owner had bottled reared her and kept her on a tether. Bless her; she thought she was a dog – a three hundred pound dog with horns! Her name had been Michelle, but I couldn't settle to the name of a former First Lady for this four-legged beastie, so we renamed her Daisy.

Daisy loved nothing more than a good scratch behind the ears or a rub on her back. She would even follow us around the field as we moved her electric fencing, giving a prod with her horns to remind us she was there and would rather like another scratch. Although I was very tolerant of Daisy, memories of Mr. Hereford were not distant enough for me to be very comfortable with her. Jimmy would often position himself between me and our oversized bovine puppy.

Daisy had been bred (in Farmer Speak) before we inherited her, meaning she was pregnant, or at least we hoped she was.

We got to know a good number of the locals at that farm, and we found more than one person who owned Dexter cattle. These are just the loveliest breed of cow, because they are really small – a very good thing in my opinion! We figured we should buy a Dexter cow as well. The chap we got Clarabelle and her baby calf, Buttercup, from had a few health issues and couldn't quite decide if he wanted to carry on with his herd or not. We were ready to buy them all if he chose "not".

Now we had three cows, and felt very farmerish. The electric fencing was proving to be somewhat inadequate though. One morning a truck pulled into our driveway and a man got out to tell us he had just stopped for a calf on the road that went past our farm. He had chased the calf back into the field for us, but thought we should know it was out. Half an hour later, another car pulled into our driveway with an alarmingly similar story. Oh dear. Buttercup was so little she was walking right under the electric wire whenever she felt like it.

Rather than risk pandemonium on our quite busy little road with a free-range calf, we got busy with a second, lower strand of electric fence, all the while being pursued and nudged by Daisy, who figured she deserved a bit more fuss than was generally being made of her.

Buttercup was contained, and Daisy delivered her first calf very successfully. He was a very beautiful Jersey boy who looked so uncannily like a deer that the children named him Buck. (It was a toss up between Buck and Bambi, but no one could agree whether Bambi was a boy or a girl. I have seen the movie many times and tried to insist that Bambi was a boy. Thumper calls him 'the young prince,' and he gets hitched to Faline, who produces twins, but my children had no interest in my Bambi trivia).

When the time came to leave our Ontario farm and make the return trip to Saskatchewan, we did not want to leave our lovely cows behind. We made arrangements to have them moved by a livestock transportation company. They set off several days ahead of us on their truck, on their way to the first of several holding facilities along the way. We'd been at our rental property a couple of weeks before they finally caught up with us. Some problem with cattle loads and an administrative mistake somewhere along the line meant our cows were stuck at their final holding facility for two weeks longer than they should have been.

We were lucky in finding the rental. It was an acreage with a barn and fencing already in place for us to house our animals. We waited eagerly for them to come home to us. The day finally came, and they were unloaded into their new small field. Jimmy and I were devastated at how thin they looked. The extended wait had taken its toll and their food rations must have been cut.

We had hauled all our own organic hay from Ontario too. Reports of the overly dry summer in Saskatchewan threatened a hay shortage that would not see our animals through the winter. We took no chances and paid rather hefty sums of money to take our own hay with us. Our August arrival meant our cows could fatten themselves back up on lush green grass, and it did not take long for them to restore to their former condition. Clarabelle even produced her second calf, a rather lovely young chap we named Banjo.

They were so restored and energized that both Daisy and Buttercup thought it would be an absolute wheeze to break through some of the fencing and run off with the neighbour's Angus bull. He was just delighted, of course! Shameless hussies!

Nine months later we were gifted with Daisy's second calf, a Jersey/Angus cross whom our youngest son named Ben, with the reasoning that both breeds were quite large, so he could be Big Ben when he was fully grown. Jimmy watched Buttercup nervously. She was barely full grown herself and the calf was unlikely to be small.

A few conversations with our local vet, and a nail-biting few days of waiting until Buttercup went into labour ("calving" remember?), we all swarmed outside to see how she was doing. It was not long before it became apparent she was not doing well at all. The vet was on standby as we had anticipated trouble. She came along with an assistant and began the procedure of a caesarian section on Buttercup.

I have had one C-section with my penultimate baby, at ten-pounds-fourteen-ounces. The doctor on shift divided his concerns between her shoulders getting stuck, because she was so big, and the fact that her head was badly positioned and needed to be manipulated around. She was presenting face-first, not crown-first. He was a very young doctor, and also male. Despite my insistence that I had delivered enough babies by this time to handle a bit of internal manipulating, (he probably could have been winched in wearing a hard hat with a yard light attached), without anesthetic, he refused point blank... unless I had an epidural put in.

Epidural anesthesia is where a long needle is inserted between two specific vertebrae of the lower spine to put a cannula into the cerebro-spinal fluid, and inject a drug that blocks all feeling in the lower body. I had one with my very first baby and I hated it so much that I had vowed I would never have another. It only worked on one side of my body, so the pain was there but lopsided. It also meant I couldn't stand up, which I desperately wanted to do. That first delivery ended up involving a huge episiotomy and a pair of forceps. Still, it seemed I had no choice but to agree.

Jimmy was standing in front of me and letting me rest my head against his chest, while I sat on the edge of the bed, a full ten centimetres dilated and having immensely powerful contractions about every thirty seconds. The anesthetist told me to hold perfectly still while he attempted to insert, in Jimmy's words, "a needle so big it could have been a hedge stake!" I couldn't hold still enough, and our baby began to show signs of distress. An emergency C-section was ordered.

So I thought I knew a thing or two about C-sections.

Nothing prepared me for the experience of a cow C-section, not that I chose to stand and watch. There seemed to be plenty of folks doing that already as our landlord had visitors at their home who thought it would be quite the thrill to crowd around a very patient vet, and entertain themselves with poor Buttercup's emergency situation.

I did pop my head around the barn doors at one point, because I couldn't stand the suspense any longer and desperately needed to know if we had a live calf, or a dead calf with a live mama, or a dead mama. It was quite the shocker to see Buttercup standing quietly against one wall of the barn with all her insides on display, and the vet shoulder-deep, firkling around for what a person could imagine might be buried treasure. Standing!

I'm not sure what I really expected to see. I mean a hospital bed was probably never an option, and a crash trolley and team of attending doctors was unlikely, but I would have thought some sterilized straw, piled high around an anesthetized, sleeping cow hooked up to an intravenous drip and draped with those nice, green surgical cloths revealing only the area to be operated on wasn't unreasonable.

Here was our young (admittedly promiscuous and arguably brought-all-this-on-herself) cow, just standing there, wide awake, on all four legs, without a hint of wobbling or passing-out, having a massive surgery on one side of her abdomen!

At one point, before she commenced the stitching-up process, our vet had Jimmy put his arm up the cow's bum so that she could thoroughly check the uterus against the resistance of his hand. Jimmy later joked that it was a first for him – to shake hands with someone else *inside* a cow.

Wobbling and passing-out was becoming a rapidly increasing probability for me, so I didn't stick around to see the much longer process of Buttercup getting sewn back together.

I have an old history with mortuary work; I am not really a squeamish person, having wheeled a two-tier trolley down a corridor that held clear-bagged sagittal (which means cut in half down the middle) human heads, and dismembered two whole human bodies into pieces that would fit into something similar to a large rubbermaid tub; but, when it comes to things that are still alive, I do get a bit wobbly.

I was once vigorously drying a glass flask in the laboratory of my first university and I'd failed to notice a crack at the rim of the flask that ran part way down in a spiral. As the knuckle of my thumb hit the crack, the glass broke and sliced my thumb knuckle down to the bone. Shocked at both the amount of blood and the sight of white bone in my own thumb, I was pretty much out for the count immediately.

That same feeling was fast approaching as I watched Buttercup, so I left the morbid rubber-necking to our uninvited guests.

***

In recent years, I can walk in the cow field without a rising sense of panic, though there are still moments when a playful steer like Buck can spook me. He did this last year when a warm sunny day in the winter seemed to inspire him to jump and skip around me as I took feed to the sheep. Jimmy, my hero husband, did his very best to shield me from the carousing Buck, but I knew he could smell my fear and delighted in it!

Just this year we have bought more cows from a dear friend and neighbour who very sensibly wants to move away from livestock and all the shenanigans that they entail. Some difficulties with a third party entrusted to care for his animals, who let them down badly, meant we took the first two cows right away to help them recover.

Betty and Boo were beautiful black Angus, both believed to have babies in their bellies, and both rather shabby looking. Betty had been bottle-reared by our friend and was a little calmer, but Boo got her name (from us) because she was very skittish and not at all keen on human contact.

Jimmy put them in the barn for a few days where they gulped down gallons of water right away, and settled to a happier life of hay on-demand and a warm place to sleep through the last of the mean winter weather. We let them outside with our small herd once they had brightened up.

They seemed to mix in reasonably well, even though they often kept to themselves. I watched them most days, and I commented to Jimmy that Betty was a bit of an odd looking thing. Her neck and head somehow seemed to be a funny shape, nothing I could name distinctly, but the lines weren't quite right. Also, both cows seemed to have bald patches. The weather was warming up, although we had a few fool's springs along the way, and we thought perhaps they were just shedding their winter coats. We'd never owned black Angus before, so we really weren't sure.

Our prized Dexter bull, Banjo, turned one year old. We decided we should try to sell him before he discovered the thing that bulls do best, and turned his affections towards female members of his own family. We have a word for that sort of thing, and it is to be discouraged in my humble opinion! We'd had a conversation or two about Betty's funny shaped head and whether some activity inside a too-close family circle had caused this in her.

Because Banjo was a very beautiful (no bias at all here!) pure Dexter, with then full organic certification, we figured it would be worth registering him and asking for top price in our sale. We approached the Canadian Dexter Association and began the gauntlet that is the registration process with the Canadian Livestock Registration Association. It took months to understand, decipher, complete, and submit an array of forms amidst which we learned we had to have him tested to prove he was what we said he was.

The tail hair test… ah… One of Banjo's endearing qualities was his shyness. If you walked right up to him, he'd walk away; if you tried to actually touch him, he'd run away! There was not a testosterone-fuelled mean bone in his body. He truly was a sweetie. Still, getting him to stand still long enough for us to snatch hairs from the end of his tail, with the roots still intact, was nothing short of a total impossibility.

Pondering how to tackle this impossible feat, I watched Banjo happily chewing his cud, and spotted a couple of small bald patches on his side towards his tail. I knew I had no chance of getting closer to him for a better look, but I showed Jimmy and shared my fear that Banjo had caught lice from Betty and Boo.

The years of parenting, and in particular when we were fostering, heralded many rounds of head lice with children at school or being swapped in and out of different homes and schools. I became skilled in the manual removal of lice, using only regular hair-conditioner and a nit comb to break the lifecycle and remove the little critters from smaller, younger heads. There's quite an art to it, and at our full capacity with eight children in our home, nit check was a regular event.

Jimmy googled cow nits, and we couldn't decide if it was the case or not. Apparently they occur round the eyes and hair loss is evident there. Betty and Boo had balding backs and rumps; their eyes were just fine.

The vet stopped by one afternoon to collect his liquid nitrogen tank which housed our remaining semen straws, and to check on poor Betty whose ear had fallen off the night before as a consequence of frost bite (itself a consequence of her poor condition). Jimmy mentioned the animals' coats and also a recent worry over Betty's knees, which seemed to be little more than a skinless scabby mess.

The vet said the word we were dreading: lice. The tiny little devils that go about the business of eating blood from their host without a care in the world were responsible for pretty much all of our new girls' problems. Worse, lice in this sense included not just external critters, the ones I am all too familiar with, but internal ones as well…meaning worms. Ugh!

I had a run-in with worms as a child, around the age of six or seven. I'd gone to the bathroom with a really itchy bum, and having had a good scratch noticed a small collection of wriggling, writhing, white, thread-like little beasties on my fingers! (Children of six or seven are still in the process of developing good hygiene practices like stopping to use bathroom tissue for such scratching occasions). I recall screaming in total horror until an adult (my dad as it happened) came in to see who was trying to murder me in our bathroom. In true dad style, he did an about-turn and called for my mum to deal with the situation.

Our whole family (we numbered a paltry four with only my sister and I as our parents' offspring) had to take worm medicine on two occasions over the next week. It was just about the most disgusting medicine on the planet, or the stuff we took back then was. Perhaps it has improved over the decades and today's victims can happily glug down whatever tasty changes to the original formula that have been thoughtfully developed.

It was called Pripsen (some seemingly minor trivia can be indelibly seared into a brain when associated with trauma). It was bright pink and could be added to either milk or water to make a drink, but after trying both versions on us, Mum realized it didn't matter what it was mixed with. It was always just vile.

My younger sister flat refused to take hers, and even though my poor mum sat with her for what seemed like hours to get her to finish it, my sister managed little more than a sip, and vomited that up straight away. To this day neither of us can even look at a strawberry milkshake.

While worrying about Banjo, fretting over Betty and Boo, and wringing our hands over the fact that by now all of our herd would have been infected, we did uncover one positive piece of news: the treatment for these parasites in cattle is a pour-on treatment that goes the length of their spine only. Wow! Where was this magic when I was a little girl? These cows don't know how lucky they are! Pour-on? That's so easy!

But, of course, it wasn't. Only Daisy is happy to have a person get up-close and personal and rub and scratch her like the dog she believes she is. It was a regular three-ring circus trying to sneak up on the rest of the cows and catch them off guard with a cup full of icy cold blue stuff to pour all the way down their backs. We enticed some into the barn with a small bucket of feed, cornered them, and wham! For all their initial panic they seemed to give the facial expression of "What? That's it?" when we finally let them back outside.

Jimmy used an old, long-handled grain scoop (the sort we used to use to snatch a cup of grain from the continuous waterfall that used to fill the auger from the tipped truck). He'd stand near the ring feeder where they would go to nibble at hay, and acting all nonchalant and pretending to be doing something very mundane, he'd quickly reach across and douse an unsuspecting cow. The precision of our applications was questionable, but we got every single one. Evidence of our success was revealed as Boo and one-eared-Betty soon began to gain weight now that the critters in their intestines that regularly robbed their food were gone.

**

Betty and Boo were the first two of the six cows destined to come our way. There was one other cow with a baby in her belly, and Jimmy needed her to deliver her calf on our farm for it to be organic. We headed out with our truck and trailer to meet our friend, and to load this next cow up from his field. He warned us she was pretty wild, but surprisingly, after only a bit of running back and forth, she went into the makeshift enclosure and climbed right into our trailer.

We felt a little smug between the three of us, but only for a few minutes, as our new girl began charging around in the confines of our tiny trailer...not even our trailer, actually; we had borrowed it. I don't know how we got her home without the whole rig tipping over.

Jimmy remains unshakably calm in situations such as these, where I lose my nerve faster than a gambler loses money. To help, he successfully engaged me in side-tracking conversation on what we should call our new cow. She was very big, bigger than any of our others so far, and a beautiful brown and cream colour, like hot chocolate. This was my first suggestion for her name, being a completely rubbish suggestion, of course. Jimmy countered with "Ovaltine", an equally delicious malted-chocolatey drink, but then rescinded it with the argument that he wasn't going to be walking the field at night calling, "Ovaltine!" any more than "Hot Chocolate!"

"What about Horlicks?"

Perfect! And my absolute favourite malted but-not-at-all-chocolate drink, and, as a bonus, we already had reached home!

I did not want to be part of getting her into the barn, where we had high hopes she would calm right down in a day or two just like her cohorts, Betty and Boo, had done. Still, I bravely stood to block the one opening she may have spied and given her best shot, and let Jimmy do everything else.

Secured in a stall, we left her and went for a coffee break. Jimmy checked on her a bit later, and came back to the house in a hurry. He'd been confused at first, because he felt pretty sure which stall he had put her in when we unloaded, and couldn't understand why she was now in a completely different stall.

It seemed Horlicks was big enough to climb right over the gate and fencing at the front of our barn stalls, and was amusing herself by climbing out of the stall we put her in, and into a new one of her choosing. It would be only a matter of time before she chose the one recently netted-in to house our hundred or so tiny baby chicks, and likely stomp all over them. We needed to let her outside.

Our herd, that had recently included Betty and Boo, were confined to a smaller area than they were used to, because of our recent tree-planting around the perimeter of our farm. Without adequate perimeter fencing to keep the cattle off the new saplings, we'd opted for temporary electric fencing on a smaller, central portion of the field.

We thought Horlicks would find Betty and Boo, recognize her old chums, and that she'd settle right down once she was outside again. We opened the barn doors to let our new girl go back into the fresh air and sunshine.

I don't know why our herd decided to leap and race all over

this cow that was clearly a head and shoulders bigger than any of them, but they did. It was like watching a rodeo. Jimmy looked on and I felt a small whimper escape my lips as Horlicks ran right through the electric fence with Buttercup hot in pursuit. The rest of the herd wisely chose not to tangle with the fence and stayed behind the now imaginary boundary we had created for them.

It was fast approaching Jimmy's afternoon bus run and we had only enough time to fix the electric fence and leave Buttercup and Horlicks to do whatever damage they would to our brand new tree line of tiny saplings in the two hours that followed. When I told the story to my friend Helen, she said when Horlicks had her calf, we should call it Moon, as in "the cow jumped over!"

Two days later, with Horlicks now comfortably settled within the confines of our temporary electric fence, we received a call from our friend telling us the three remaining cows, (young heifers in Farmer Speak, which means girl cows that have not had any babies yet), had all broken through the fence over at his field and run off into the neighbour's trees.

We'd arranged to go and collect more big round bales of hay from another neighbour. With no rain at all so far that spring, there was just no grass for our cows to eat. Between the growing number of cattle and the sheep (with their super-fast growing lambs!), we were rapidly going through hay bales. We promised to go right over and help round up the escapees once we'd loaded the hay.

When we got there, it was decided that the job would need many more bodies. We all agreed to leave the wanderers where they were until after school, when our two families combined could produce a small army of children to run around and herd up the energetic young beasties.

That evening, when Jimmy returned, he became concerned for one of the young cows, Horlicks' first calf. She had a big gob of mucus-like slime and water hanging out of her rear end. This sort of thing usually only happens when an amniotic sac is starting to pop out, and an amniotic sac will only exist if there is a baby in there. Oh no. It would seem this particular young lady had done the very same thing our two shameless hussies had done almost two years earlier – run off with a bull –but in her case she had managed to get herself pregnant at around six months (six months!) of age. This was not going to end well.

We headed over in the morning, right after Jimmy's morning bus run, even leaving our own flocks, broods, and herds without their breakfast to go and see our youngster. She was not well at all. Our friend had been with her on and off since the day before. Her baby calf had one leg and a head out, but was stuck fast and quite clearly dead. We had taken water, soap, lubricant, ropes, iodine, and towels – everything we could think of that might be useful – but within a short space of time it became clear none of these things would be necessary.

It is so very sad when these things happen, but every farmer must weigh his options when situations become bleak. With a small, outside chance of saving the heifer involving a vet bill, surgery, and no guarantee that shock or infection wouldn't take her anyway, and with honest acknowledgement of the fact that we raise these phenomenal animals to be slaughtered and eaten in the end, the most obvious choice was to skip the hassle, headache, and expense, and use the bullet brought along as a last resort. Her carcass was butchered, and a fair amount of meat salvaged.

We had taken our trailer along, with a thought to bringing home all three heifers, and alleviate the problems our friend was having. It seemed sensible to load up the two remaining girls, who were the first calves of Betty and Boo. Jimmy named them Billie and Bobby, not overdoing the 'B' letter at all!

Naturally, they had other ideas. Across this particular field were areas of semi-dense brush and tree growth. This pair of tinkers seemed to know exactly how difficult it would be for us grown humans to fight our way into the scratchy branches to move them on and towards our waiting trailer. They'd almost tag-team one another.

I could imagine the dialogue being telepathically communicated between them: "I'll go to the middle and face one way; you skirt around me and face the other. They'll never get us to go out in the same direction!"

They would stoically lodge themselves right in the centre of the prickliest bushes and no amount of shouting or clapping would move them, only climbing in there risking the loss of an eye and half a shirt would get them out. It was rinse-and-repeat the whole half mile or so.

Finally, loaded and back at our place, we got them inside the barn to be wormed just like we had treated all our other cattle. They were both about as feisty as Horlicks was, throwing random kicks at Jimmy and at the wall in their stall. They managed to kick hard enough that a broom fell and a cupboard door got shocked open spilling the cupboard's contents all over the tack room floor, which was at the other end of the barn. Bloody hell!

Once outside and re-acquainted with their mothers and the rest of our herd, Billie and Bobby (occasionally referred to as Thing One and Thing Two with their scruffy coats and nervous, shifty eyes) calmed right down, just as Horlicks had.

Boo was the first to have her calf that spring. The children named her Kitty, after the partnership of Kitty and Boo in the Monsters, Inc. movie from 2001. Despite her shyness and distrust of all things two-legged, Jimmy did manage to get them into the barn for a couple of nights to ensure all was well with mother and baby.

Boo went ballistic at our free-range barn chickens, cornering one so fast Jimmy didn't have chance to intervene before she stood on its leg injuring the poor bird such that it limped for several days afterwards.

Boo was delighted to be released back outside with her calf, just in time for Clarabelle to be brought in with her new bundle of joy. This little boy was born on Mother's Day and I suggested Emdy for its name, as in M.D. for Mother's Day. (See, all those university degrees do pay off once in a while!)

Third on the birthing rotation was Betty, our one-eared unfortunate, but she delivered a healthy little girl who was named Nyx by our son's friend at school. Frankly, with nothing but Black Angus springing forth from each bovine uterus, it was getting tricky to tell one animal from another with names becoming a paperwork detail only.

Horlicks made us wait a whole week after Nyx arrived. Jimmy was fretting about trying to get her in the barn again, memories of last time were still pretty raw! The weather had been very warm, but a cold spell was forecast with an ice storm, high winds, and rain.

Jimmy and I arrived home from fetching hay bales from a neighbour one morning to see Horlicks standing at the furthest point in the field from shelter with a small black bundle at her feet. She was tenderly licking her new infant in the cold and wet hail shower. Oh Horlicks! Could you not have considered the well being of your new charge, plopped out from a warm and snug place that was full-on body temperature to a miserable cold, wet, windy drizzle of frozen water pellets? Why did you not go to the shelter at the side of the barn?

She allowed us to approach, perhaps feeling genuinely confused by what had just happened at her rear end. Little Moon was shivering and still very wet. Jimmy carried her all the way back to the shelter at the barn, and called Horlicks to follow. But the geographical place of her delivery seemed to be imprinted on Horlicks' brain. She wouldn't follow, and any steps away from that spot were followed by a swift return to it.

The calf was warmer out of the wind, but still wet. We dried her with straw, careful not to taint her own smell with the detritus we carry on our gloves. Jimmy called Horlicks for a good few minutes before deciding to leave her a while to see if she could figure things out for herself. By mid-afternoon he took Moon (in a wheelbarrow this time, smart thinking!) back up the field to where her mother still stood. He used the barrow to create a makeshift windbreak against the worst of the cold, and left them to it.

For several days we would watch the little calves curl up in what barely passed as brush or scrub for shelter, while mamas roved about grazing. Moon always seemed to be further out than the others, and even when Jimmy would get her up and drive her (using her own legs by now) to the shelter for protection, she inevitably found her way back out to a spot totally exposed to the elements, which at that time were notably unfavourable. It seemed Moon wasn't very smart.

It was a Tuesday morning when Jimmy went out to set off on his morning bus run. One of our daughters was at the window, and commented that dad had walked to the pasture, rather than to his bus. I rushed out to see what was wrong.

Jimmy spends a lot of time checking the status quo outside when he does his 5:00am milking routine. Something must be wrong for him to be out there again when he should be steering his bus out of the driveway. And something was wrong. Moon lay dead in the middle of the pasture.

We hadn't lost a calf before. Jimmy had lost many, during his time on his old family farm in England when his father was a dairy farmer, but none since we have farmed together. It was a sad moment.

It was also sad to watch Horlicks bellow and bellow for a calf that she couldn't find. Jimmy wanted to try and milk her by hand, knowing how sore she would be after those few days of feeding. I have regaled him many times with what it feels like to be engorged and suffer mastitis as a lactating mammal! But Horlicks was still wild enough to tolerate no such effort from him.

The week before we lost Moon, we had indulged at a local Garden Centre, buying fruit trees, roses, and juniper shrubs. The trees were planted already, and two of the roses had gone into a perennial patch of our produce garden; only two junipers and two rose bushes remained to be given their forever-home.

Moon had been dead for about twenty-four hours. It seemed the perfect solution to distribute her as plant food between the holes our tractor-powered auger would create. I had a reputation for butchering during our lambing season, as you already know, carving up those that did not survive and serving them to our pigs.

We moved her carcass to a bare patch of soil in the smaller of our garden plots. I had raked away topsoil and wood chips, planning to re-cover the area after our butchering operation to conceal any spilled blood. I had a sharpened kitchen knife, and I tasked Jimmy with a wood saw to cut through bone when I had removed enough skin and soft tissue. It didn't take very long at all. We cut her into eight pieces: four legs, her head, and three sections of her body. Each of our four augered holes was filled partway up with two separate body parts. Enough room remained for some back-fill of soil, and then our shrubs and bushes were to be planted over the top.

I love the Circle of Life philosophy. Moon will give minerals, elements, and molecules of her body to feed and enrich the soil our new plants would grow from. Her decomposition is the greatest gift to our earth. Jimmy took a moment to explain to Horlicks all the good things her baby was now doing when he went to the barn that afternoon.

I have had similar conversations with my own children about when my time of death comes around. I have been a fan of organ donation all my life, and registered each of my children from the time they were born. Perhaps it sounds cold, but my first degree was in Biology. I understand life and death. I want my minerals, elements, and molecules to do something good. The thought of encasing them in a highly varnished, ornate box that leaches toxic volatile organic compounds into the soil and preserves my remains for years and years, strikes me as totally mad.

I even contacted our local city cemetery, learning along the way that Canadian law states a person does not have to be buried in a coffin. Were there 'green plots' available? To be buried in just a shroud would be my preference. It was a "no" sadly, but my hope is that will change by the time I die. I have all the forms to donate my body to a local university, just like the one I used to work at all those years ago, but I am torn between making myself a useful resource for medical students, dentists, and so-on, and being embalmed to the point where I am toxic, volatile, organic compounds, doing no good at all, as I leach into the surrounding earth. It's a conundrum I will continue to ponder, especially as I review my wine consumption which may be serving as a long-term substitute for that extensive embalming anyway!

***

Jimmy had an offer from our former landlords; grass. We were struggling so much with limited pasture on our new farm. The land we had inherited through buying our new place was far from 'green and pleasant'. The space we used to rent before completing the purchase of this farm had grass-a-plenty. Would we be willing to transport a few cows over there and help those folks get on top of almost seventeen acres of long grass? Well, yes we would!

Jimmy took just over half of our cattle in July. He phoned regularly and sauntered over there to say 'hi' every so often. Buck and Ben would recognise him instantly and come over for a rub. Horlicks remained somewhat aloof, but she'd come close enough to indicate it was good to see Jimmy again.

A long and incredibly hot and dry summer gave us the relentless task of moving electric fence for the cattle we had left at home. Grass just refused to regenerate itself in the absence of rain. It meant we had to keep moving our group along to give them access to some previously unmunched grass.

The first time around Jimmy tackled the job alone, and shut

the cows into the sheep corral to keep them from wandering off while the fence was down. It is a difficult job for one man to do by himself. The second time around I helped him out, and we chose to take a bit of a gamble with our partial herd. They were all up close to the barn, lying down and chewing their cud, looking like they'd had a decent meal and were taking an afternoon rest. We figured if we started at the top of the fenced area, about a quarter of a mile away from them, we'd be safe enough to drop the fence line unnoticed. Wrong! Our cattle are pretty smart, and knew straight away that we were about to move the fence to offer up some lush and tasty new grass. They roused themselves from their restful cud-chewing daze and thundered up the field towards us and the obvious promise of food.

Jimmy said to rattle the wires that were lying on the ground thinking that might be enough to warn them off. It worked for all of thirty seconds until Buttercup, with bold and gay abandon, simply stepped right over the wires and set right to the task of chomping on the lovely, long grass.

We had enough of the fence down to move the whole rig sideways a few feet, allowing everyone some of the new grass, but Buttercup was still on the wrong side of the wire. We tried lifting it over the top of her, skipping-rope style, but she was having none of that. It took several attempts of a carefully orchestrated pincer manoeuvre to herd her back over the wire to join her friends.

There were third and fourth times around too. Were we ever thankful when late August finally brought us some rains.

***

I manage a stall at Farmers' Market, two stalls in fact: one at our lovely local holiday town of Regina Beach, and one in the capital city of Regina, Saskatchewan.

One of our valued customers recently wrote to us via email with a complaint about the store prices of steak, asking if we could offer a better deal to her.

I've had a really hard time thinking of the right response.

Buck was our very first calf. Buck was our very first butchered-for-beef animal. I have such mixed emotions.

I have a photo of that Bambi-look alike from the day he was born. He has travelled across Canada to remain with us, and has been a feature on our farms and in our lives for two years.

Being born on our farm meant Buck was also the first animal to qualify for 'certified organic' status. Even though we ended up not listing our animals in our production plan, they are all fed, housed, and cared for to organic standards. We transported our own hay across Canada when we left Ontario, to be sure Buck and all of our cattle had organic hay to eat. We have travelled four-hour round-trips up to Saskatoon to purchase organically approved minerals for our cattle. We had to source organic hay the next two seasons, because we didn't have any of our own, and we travelled fair distances and paid heavily to do so.

This last season Jimmy found a local source, and became involved in the process of haymaking in order to manage and off-set the high costs of buying. In fact, we all became involved in the process! As trailer load after trailer load arrived back at our farm, it was necessary to move the little square bales from the trailer to the attic of the barn.

On a couple of these occasions, Jimmy and I have accomplished this by ourselves. He pitches the bales up through the loft doorway, literally throwing them, one after another, using a pitchfork when the level he is working from drops so low that he cannot throw high enough without the fork. I have the less strenuous task of moving them away from the loft doorway and onto an appropriate stack. I say less strenuous, because technically it is, but with all things considered and using my own (weary) perspective rather than that of an objective observer, I have to say it is still plenty strenuous, thank you very much!

We would haul almost a hundred bales in an hour. One delivery included some densely-packed and seriously heavy bales, and we used a rig we had been gifted in the loft of our barn, by the former owners, called a bale-lift. It was brilliant! With our two younger boys helping, we managed a hundred and fifty rather heavy bales in just over an hour!

Before Buck and the other grazers went back to our old rental property for some 'lawn-mowing', Jimmy discovered Buck not only enjoys a good head scratch, but will lift his hind leg for an inner-thigh scratch too. Visiting the animals regularly at our old rental property, Buck would always recognise Jimmy and play the scratching game.

We have gone to great lengths and great expense to give all

of our animals the best life we possibly can. They are a part of our family, even though we know and understand their purpose as food. In that purpose though, is our livelihood. There could never be any part of Buck that could be called cheap meat. So to answer the email I received, "No. I can't offer a better price, but I certainly can offer better quality of meat worth more than the dollar you might pay for it, in my humble opinion."

Daisy was due to produce her next calf by the middle of September. Debate over who else might be butchered to combat the challenges invoked by another dry season next year have continued. Our cowing adventures have been very ambitious indeed… and I'm quite certain will continue to be!

PART 4

Greening

I love seeds! I love buying them, saving them, and stealing them. Well, by stealing, I really mean taking them mostly with permission, even if sought after the fact.

We had been in a rental property for just over a year between farms. I merrily gathered flower head seeds from both our own plants, in case they didn't make it through the winter after down-grading a few climate zones, and the plants already established at the rental property. I was only part way through my indulgent pilfering when it occurred to me that I should have asked the property owners first. The phrase "it is easier to seek forgiveness than to ask permission" popped into my conscience, and I made a mental note to enlighten the landlord when I next saw him.

I had tried growing vegetables from seeds several times from an English allotment more than a decade earlier (with my gardening implements balanced on the axles of an old-fashioned carriage pram that transported a water bottle, a snack, and one very young baby) to Canadian farms in both Saskatchewan and Ontario. It was certainly not the first time I have fretted over sorry-looking seedlings that are starved of the light they require, crammed onto windowsills and stuffed, wobbly shelving housing.

If I'm honest, my seed germinating endeavours have come a long way.

Jimmy and I encountered soil-block-making for the first time in Ontario; simultaneously through my volunteer gardening work with a local community garden, and from the wisdom of Eliot Coleman in a book. Making soil blocks is a lot like making sand castles really, but smellier.

There are a variety of recipes out there, and we tried several. Jimmy was horrified at actually buying a bag of sheep manure, having grown up on an English dairy farm. The idea of paying for muck was absurd to him. But there we were, new to that farm, without any form of poo-producing beasties to help us out. Purchasing poo was our only option.

That year I loaded a four-tier two-foot by two-foot shelf system, first with a layer of waterproof plastic, and then with an absorbent water blanket that would wick water from a reservoir (which I didn't have) underneath all the soil blocks.

This would provide an ongoing supply of moisture through the bottom of the block. In the absence of a reservoir, I just used a watering can to keep the blankets wet. It wasn't ideal since the moisture levels were not consistent, but I was determined to make do with what I had.

The first round of soil blocks were popped out of a twenty-block mould and were little tiny things about three quarters of an inch square. The mould put a dent in the top of each block, a small divet to drop a seed into. Germination was pretty good in general (depending on the age of the seeds), and it was pure joy to watch those little sproutlings grow!

It was not very long, however, before the not-so-little sproutlings needed a bit more room. The next stage was potting on, or "blocking on" I suppose, where I would take the three-quarter-inch square block with the sprout and drop it into a two inch square soil block, giving it more room to grow.

Although this mould only popped out four blocks at a time, it very cleverly added a perfect three quarter inch cube-shaped indent so that I could just drop that original block straight into it!

The down side is that two inch blocks take up considerably more space than their three-quarter-inch predecessors, so it was impossible to have the same number of plants in the same space. Our early starters of pepper, tomato, and cabbage needed more room... a lot more room!

Our time at that farm was truly blessed by the wonderful friends and neighbours we had there. It seemed any time we even had a thought that we needed something, someone would show up with an item remarkably close to the thing we were lacking. In this case, it turned out to be an old tubular metal frame for a temporary covered structure (think of a garage but made to look like a tent). It seemed an ideal makeshift greenhouse!

Jimmy and I wrapped the frame in vapour membrane, the sort used in housebuilding here in North America, pieced together with tuck-tape. In record time Jimmy knocked up a frame to support an old set of patio doors that had also been gifted to us, and voila! Our first greenhouse ever!

We moved the seedlings out even though it was only March. My volunteer gardening had imparted the wisdom of thermal mass to regulate temperature fluctuations; large 45-gallon containers filled with water will store heat from the sun during the day and slowly release it through the night. We used six oil drums painted black, and placed them in a line down the middle of our precarious polythene shack. Slatted-board structures (also knocked up in record time by Jim) were placed over the top of the drums. Plastic sheeting and a large water blanket topped it off, with one end dangling into the drum of water below it. It is quite remarkable how far that wicking action will go, but to be on the safe side, we dipped the water blanket into its nearest drum at each end of our table.

Seedlings were carefully transported in boxes, to reduce the shock of the environmental change from cozy-Aga-warm kitchen and dining room windows to the questionable-looking plastic-and-red-tape shed with nothing but barrels of cold water for any vague promise of warmth.

We had thermometers that would record minimum and maximum temperatures, and it was a huge surprise that our seedlings actually survived when night time temperatures dropped to around fifteen degrees below zero! We would tuck them in each night, with a large six-inch-tall cardboard collar that ran around all the seedlings on the table, and a layer of plastic placed over the top of them like a really dismal sort of a duvet.

Through the month of March we lost a handful of the plants that were on the corners of the table to frost, but the bulk of our efforts were a roaring success.

The final stage of blocking-on was to place the 2 inch square blocks with their little plants into hefty four-inch cubes, also cleverly produced with a precise two-inch cube indent to accommodate the previous stage. This mould is a one-block at a time producer, making the sandcastle-fun quickly disappear into laborious repetition to match the number of seedlings we had.

Space was getting tight again, and we regularly sent up silent prayers for the season to get a bloody move on. Even in Ontario there was caution against planting too much outside before the end of May, as an unwelcome surprise night frost would see off any tender little plants without the slightest remorse.

Finally, the opportunity came to stick our growing darlings into the ground. I had somehow ended up with well over one hundred tomato plants. It was the first year we had cultivated a garden patch in what was formerly something in between lawn and rough pasture.

We divided up the excessive number of tomato plants between the new garden and the ground inside the greenhouse. In the latter case, I had crowded the plants in so tightly that even though they grew to over eight feet tall and produced prolific and abundant fruits, it was impossible to get to all the tomatoes, because the vines were a decent representation of a dense, machete-requiring jungle. Conversely, the field tomatoes (as I believe is the appropriate term for plants just doing their thing on open ground) that had all the space in the world around them, just didn't seem to fancy throwing off many tomatoes. Those that did appear were quickly bitten into by a variety of local rodents and ambushing critters.

There's some theory on 'pinching out' side growth on tomato vines, but I lived in constant fear of picking the wrong bit off and killing my plant. Yes, my plants had side growth, up growth, and around growth aplenty. This may not have helped the fruiting situation upon reflection, but I feel the genius of soil-blocking and thermal mass was enough elevated wisdom and superior knowledge for one season; stupidity and ignorance could reign supreme over much of the remaining tasks.

Amongst the greenhouse-dwelling thicket were my pepper and eggplant varieties. I had boldly purchased four Trinidad Scorpion Pepper plants, since I am a big fan of all things hot-and-spicy. The catalogue I selected them from gave a DEFCON-one level warning for the peppers this plant would produce.

Pepper heat is measured in Scoville units. The average jalapeno might score a few hundred units of heat, but this bad boy was well over a million! Those plants provided more hot peppers than I could count. But at that heat, I hadn't really thought through what I was actually going to do with them. I threw the lot into the deep freeze figuring I'd think of something eventually.

Sometime later that season I pulled out one chili, one chili, and made a very large stock pot of coconut and lime curry. It was absolutely delicious, but felt like lava on the tongue and down the throat; utterly inedible. The rest of the pepper bounty stayed in that deep freeze for a further two years.

I had read something in the catalogue I bought them from about how best to utilise such fiery fruit, but couldn't quite remember. It was two years later as we moved farms, that I had the opportunity to order from that same catalogue again. Now, I could read the information about what to do with my Trinidad Scorpion peppers.

The advice was to make a hot sauce with them, rather than try to eat them. One only needed to fill a bottle with peppers, add lime juice, vodka, or vinegar, and just keep refilling the liquid, using the same peppers over and over. I had frozen the molten lava curry I made, too, in small batches that I could add to a larger quantity of non-spicy sauce. It worked quite well, and the newly-diluted curry was pretty good.

I decided to try the hot sauce suggestion. I spent an afternoon chopping the frozen chillies into small strips that would fit through the narrow necks of the bottles. A bit like a wine bottle in size, I filled three bottles to about one third full. At the same time I popped peppers into a larger, old syrup container, to make what I nicknamed 'gopher burn', a hot pepper spray to apply to my garden to try and keep the gophers off my baby plants later in spring. Choosing to amalgamate all the options suggested in the catalogue, rather than selecting just one (which I suspect was their intention), I added the juice of half a dozen limes between all three bottles, and a good 200ml of vodka to each, with a top-up of water and a spoonful of salt. The 'gopher burn' got white vinegar and rubbing alcohol as I figured I wasn't going to squander tasty limes or decent vodka on our resident rodents.

I felt pretty accomplished as evening rolled around and I set my three bottles in our cold room to mature for a month or three, when I noticed something was wrong with my hands. My fingers had turned an odd purplish-red and had tiny white and red marks all over them. I felt like I'd stripped off skin in an acid bath or something. A consultation with Dr. Google informed me that the Scoville units I had been working with serve to burn skin and create minute blisters just as if I'd stuck my hand on a hot plate! It took two days and several applications of shea butter to get them to calm down. I should have worn gloves! A quick peek back at that catalogue said exactly that: "Do not handle with bare hands. Wear gloves!"

The hoop house we brought with us from Ontario needed to be erected to commence transplanting our seed blocks to larger ones. The dates were circled (in pencil only, but definitely circled) and the volunteers were organized. I had even bought burgers and buns to supply outdoor barbecue food, because of the Covid social distancing restrictions.

Then, the temperature dropped, snow fell, and the wind howled. I looked at my poor sad seedlings, all leggy and reaching like gangly, stringy things towards the modicum of light available to them. I sighed a big sigh (which I like to think was the equivalent of a hug to little seedlings as it is loaded with carbon dioxide which they really love). I explained how sorry I was that they would not find plant-peace in the form of bigger soil-blocks to stretch their cramped roots in, and have day-long exposure to the sun's cheery rays beneath the protective layer of double-skin polythene with the assurance of enduring warmth, supplied by thermal mass in the form of 45-gallon drums filled with water that did double duty to supply them with a continuous water source too. No. Instead they could only remain exactly where they were, and continue to reach and suffer cramped toes.

The following week, things began to look up again. Warmer weather arrived that brought the bees to life with gusto! We were rather behind on our preparations, and didn't want to call in those wonderful volunteers until we had everything ready.

***

When we bought this farm we were so very excited; our early expectations in moving back to Saskatchewan included the idea that we would purchase land only (we were looking for a quarter section, 160 acres) and tolerate the torture of living in an RV or mobile home of some sort for two or more years, while we built a farmhouse and outbuildings for ourselves. It was a big stretch for our budget, but imagine our joy when we managed to find a quarter section of land in the area we wanted to relocate to with a house and buildings already on it, and perimeter fencing too!

Moving from an ample, century-old, five bedroom farmhouse into a small two bedroom dwelling was a challenge, but the house was in reasonable condition, with electricity, running water, and (mostly) flushing toilets. It was a big jump on the caravan-in-a-field scenario that we were expecting.

The previous owners had built an expansive deck across the whole east side of the house, very lovely, but really not a big requirement for us. However, since the pandemic had driven timber prices into silly numbers, we figured we could repurpose all those yards of marvellous deck lumber into a few different applications.

We began dismantling the deck in our first fall season, saving every inch of timber and every screw. Jimmy actually did a few repairs and restorations to give us the benefit of half of the original deck for the remainder of that fall season. We enjoyed a glass of wine or two in the warm evenings and a barbecued meal or two on the very well-constructed outdoor space, but that next spring the remainder came down. We selected just the right planks to build the foundation bars for our hoop house, even re-using those saved screws!

Our pigs had done a fine job in the previous six months of 'piggivating' a decent sized garden plot, which we could use to grow our market garden vegetables. The soil was rich and dark, with a healthy dose of composted straw (the pigs' winter duvet in their Jimmy-made shelter). We kept the pigs inside an electric chicken fence enclosure; pigs do not know that they are not chickens, nor do they seem to distinguish between types of fencing. We managed to contain them when they were really small with just two strands of electric wire, but we learned the hard way when they figured a quick zap was worth it for free reign over the entire yard!

Electric chicken fence is a visible mesh with current running through every other strand. In the depths of winter with snow drifts higher than the fence itself, the current was virtually nothing, but the pigs could still see the fence. On only one occasion, when the high drifts were made very firm by freeze/thaw temperatures, did they climb right out of their enclosure. Jimmy just took two buckets of their feed and walked over the same drifts to guide them straight back in! Then, he quickly fetched a shovel and removed the escape route.

I had ordered 5750 trees from the local Provincial Initiative that provides free trees and shrubs for farm shelterbelts, riparian buffers, and wildlife habitats. What arrived the following spring was pretty much half of what I had ordered. Due to COVID restrictions, I was informed, there were less trees planted and some species were not planted at all. (Our neighbours tell us they only ever receive half of what they order.) Still, the better part of three thousand trees arrived in eight different boxes that needed collecting during the last week of April.

We had organized the loan of a tractor-pulled tree planter from our local township office, and we were all set to go!

The week of extensive tree planting coincided with the

week of almost a hundred one-day-old birds arriving, both conspiring to put our hoop house construction on hold. This meant extended suffering for my sorry-looking windowsill seedlings. No doubt the little saplings could have remained bundled inside their boxes for a short while, while we prioritized the hoop house, but it's a tough call to gamble on the rate of deterioration of so many trees, who would additionally benefit from any early spring rain that came our way. Thus, tree planting trumped blocking of sad-but-surviving seedlings that would only be upgraded from windowsill to polythene tube, and eventually bigger soil blocks. Rome never seems to get built in a day, does it?

We had our dear friend Helen volunteer to help us for our first afternoon around the two-mile perimeter of our farm, and all four of our youngest children worked in earnest alongside us for the whole afternoon.

The tree planter could sit two people, one on either side, for dropping saplings into the furrow made by the digging part, as well as hold full boxes and tools for the duration of the journey.

We made space for a third person to sit in the most uncomfortable manner imaginable too, right between the two seats. There, they could help unwrap bundles, load the feet-level trays, and generally make sure each sapling was in the ground the right way up and going through the presser wheels in the right way, rather than getting run over and squished by them, which seemed to be the tree planter's preferred method of operating.

Our first pass was the outermost row of trees. These species are put there to cope with the initial blast of prairie storms, from wind to hail to blizzards. They are robust chaps, and I had selected Jack Pine and White Spruce for the job. They are spaced apart by twelve feet, making the going pretty easy for those folks perched on the tree planter, and even as the person walking behind and checking the plants after they had been put into the soil. This was my job, and included hilling up extra dirt if a little rootstock was still visible, righting any skewed specimens, and firming soil when needed. I enjoyed a leisurely pace and secretly imparted love and blessings on every little tree I encountered.

Our difficulty was in the poorly prepared soil, and the determinedly wonky penchant of the tree planter. Stops to unblock great gobs of sod, root mass, and mud were frequent. Jimmy had been over our mapped tree lines a couple of times with his tractor-pulled rototiller, but hampered by weather and a million other demands on our new farm, he did not make the number of passes we needed. To say the ground was rough was an understatement. Helen and Jimmy were both at one point walking on either side of the tree planter, vigorously hacking away at the build-up of field matter with a crowbar and a spade, to allow the machine to progress. We ended up by-passing large stretches of the outermost row, and kept around 200 trees in the box, to tackle later.

Midway through our endeavours, we found the need for sustenance and bathroom breaks too overwhelming to ignore. We all piled into the truck that had been accompanying us around the field with the supply of boxed trees, additional tools, clothing, coats, gloves, drinks, and so-on. The eldest of our four younger children was driving the truck, and Jimmy and I ended up sitting in the back seat together, which is an event so rare it is noteworthy!

Not one to miss a trick, Helen leaned around from her front passenger seat and shouted, "No necking!" which made me giggle and Jimmy feign ignorance by asking what necking was. He then reached over to tickle my neck with his fingers saying, "Do you mean this, Helen?" She laughed out loud, and said he had to at least leave a hickey.

We fuelled-up on Helen's very delicious homemade vegetable brownies (made with rhubarb and zucchini), set supper to heat in the oven on a low light, and made our way back to the field to continue battle with machinery and earth.

The last leg of our perimeter was torture. This was the part that involved all that vigorous hacking. It seemed like we had to stop to de-clog the planter after every single tree it put in the soil. Halfway down the north side, we quit. The view of our yard in front of us was enough of an inspiration for us to cave into the promise of a glass of wine… or three… and leave the rest until the next day.

I stumbled out of bed the next morning feeling like I had tackled and wrestled all twenty of our pigs, with aches in muscles I didn't know I had, and joints feeling like they could do with a grease gun, or a quick squirt of oil at the very least!

This day had as many treats in store as the last one. Our eldest daughter came out to help us in the afternoon. The day was much cooler, and out in the open field it got pretty cold. We had taken extra clothing and layers in the truck, but not enough.

Our first mission was to plant the innermost row. These were very small saplings of Buffaloberry, Siberian Crab Apple, and Red Osier Dogwood. They are planted much closer together with only three feet between each one. We had not set the planter deep enough, but I didn't realize this right away, believing the first couple of trees had just somehow missed the presser wheels. I walked back to the yard and our garden shed to fetch my trowel that had been forgotten in the clamour to pack water bottles and toques.

By the time I returned to that first row, the tractor had pulled the tree planter quite a long way ahead without a single sapling actually in the ground. I began digging each plant in, but quickly realized if I did not alert the tractor driver, Jimmy, in that precise moment, I'd end up planting 2 miles of trees by hand.

I'd already shed my coat and shirt; even in cool and windy conditions a body heats up rather quickly when manually planting with a small hand trowel! Using the trowel as a marker, I ran ahead up the gentle rise of our field to spy the blundering machinery over the crest of the hill.

Knowing Jimmy would not hear me above the loud and steady chugging of our cherished old International 454, I started waving my arms frantically and shouting. (Funny how I couldn't help but shout anyway, even though I knew I wouldn't be heard.) Whether it was the windmill arms, or some keen ear caught the deranged howling of a mad woman, or whether it was pure coincidence that someone turned in my direction, I don't know. But, mercifully, the tractor stopped and I was able to run (and when I say run I mean more like huff, wheeze, and stagger) forwards to the rest of our group to tell them, between gasps, that whilst I don't mind re-planting odd mishaps, there was no way I intended to do the whole row while the tree planter glibly and randomly threw saplings onto the ground in vaguely the right spot.

Adjustments were made to the digging-earth-part as I turned away to find my trowel, chuntering and mumbling under my breath. It was quite a lot of minutes later when I had found my way back to the crest of the hill, that I saw the lurching and lolloping machinery had not made much progress at all. In fact, the entire group was on their hands and knees looking for all the world like someone had lost a contact lens, and would be unable to continue until it was found amongst the dust, clods, and mud.

The searching was so earnest, I couldn't help but ask, "What did you lose?"

"The plants!" replied our youngest daughter. "We can't find the plants!"

Indeed, I looked back to where I had stopped my re-planting. She was right. There wasn't a single plant to be seen. The digging-earth-part had been set too low and had completely buried every seedling under the presser wheels. I joined in the searching, giving up my former rage against the inept too-shallow planting machine, to a new rage against the inept too-deep planting machine. For goodness sake, I could probably plant the row twice over by hand in the time this rig was taking!

There are times I am endeared by Jimmy's attention to detail (of course there are times I am frustrated beyond words by it, but this was not one of those times). Where I would have rather sloppily guessed at three-foot spacings, Jimmy insisted we use the measuring wheel, at least for the first while, until we established a rhythm. Each time we uncovered a buried sapling, we knew exactly where to look for the next one. It was less trying-to-find-a-needle-in-a-haystack, and more here-are-the-GPS-coordinates-for-your-needle. Bravo, Jimmy!

It seemed to take forever, but finally we had some bottoms back in the tree planter seats. We were off again, temporarily.

What in wet years would have qualified as a slough, we were now in a dense, boggy, heavy soil that clogged and stuck the planter, tipping it at precarious angles. It caused no end of frustration as we futilely unblocked it and tried again.

Jimmy had the idea of tackling the row from the other way on, thinking perhaps the slope of the land would be more beneficial coming from the other direction. With nothing to lose, quite frankly, we decided to give it a try.

Jimmy set off with the digging-earth-part raised high and out of the soil to reposition himself at the far end of that east pass. It seemed to be my turn to fetch and move the truck. I was happy enough to oblige and experience just a momentary respite from being bent double over the ground.

Revelling in the comfort of an actual chair and the warm confines of the vehicle, I saw with horror a scene unfolding before me, played out almost as if in slow motion. Our youngest daughter had positioned herself as that third person on the awkward part of the tree planter that is between the two actual planting seats. As the tractor ambled up the slope, she had her feet on the ground in front of the presser wheels 'walking' them to match the slow speed of the moving machinery. I learned later that there was a small hump in the ground, just enough to bump the tractor over, and just enough to catch her foot as it passed beneath her. In less than a second, the presser wheels had snatched her foot and dragged her leg underneath the planter.

Driving directly behind I could see her go down. I'm not sure how I managed to apply the brakes of the truck and leap out of the driver's door so fast, but I was running to get to her even before my eldest daughter and one of our sons had begun shouting "Stop!" to Jimmy. He later calculated it took him four feet to come to a complete halt.

I feared the worst. Her face was a mask of shock, and her whole leg was wedged underneath the planter, which try as I might, I couldn't lift by myself. It took only a second for Jimmy to fly off his seat and join our son and me around the planter. We managed to lift it together, and pull her out.

I expected a rag-doll floppy child with a shattered leg and many weeks in hospital in front of us. My hands were shaking so badly that when I held her in my arms, I think I was actually making her vibrate. But she stood perfectly well, and even walked with me back to the truck which was not very far from the halted machinery.

We pulled her shoe and sock off and lifted one leg of her pants to view the damage; some serious bruising and wheel marks, some nasty abrasions on the leg and on her arm, but miraculously, no serious damage. Still shaking badly, I only just managed to get her sock back on. She got to rest easy in the truck after that!

Being one person down in our team meant we couldn't manage all the different jobs quite as well. And when one child needed the bathroom back at the house, it meant half the team would be gone just to get him there.

It was our son who had the brilliant idea of teaching his not-as-injured-as-we-feared younger sister to drive the truck herself. And so, it was towards the end of the afternoon, that Jimmy experienced the rather odd situation of being driven across our field by his thirteen year old daughter!

The temperature dropped, and we all began feeling very chilly. The youngest of our helpers were delighted to be chauffeured around by their underage, but oh-so-willing driver, and had taken to simply hanging-out in the warm truck rather than sitting on the very cold tree planter as it was dragged around the last stretch of our field. My eldest daughter and I took a deep breath and nobly seated ourselves down to be pulled along by Jimmy on the tractor.

Our fingers were blue and we couldn't feel our toes. We also were getting very hungry! I even offered to shut the operation down and call it a day, but bless her, our eldest daughter had not come all the way out to us to quit.

On we went! It meant we had no keen and vigilant walkers behind us though; no one to check if our little saplings were going in the right way up (or even going in at all!)

The tree planter still seemed to have mood swings of its own and chose running-over rather than planting. We were cold, hungry, and tired, but I figured we'd just get the job done and go back to check for casualties another day.

The triumph of planting the last tree was resounding! Our group charged en-masse to the house for a hot meal and a very much needed glass of wine!

It wasn't quite the last tree though. We had the box of Jack Pine and White Spruce that did not fit into the outermost row, and I found a solitary bundle of Siberian Crab Apple that had somehow remained hidden and were missed in the planting process.

Helen offered to come out and help me finish the job a couple of days later. We took a different approach, having returned the tree planter back to our township office. We loaded a wheelbarrow and headed out on foot, beginning at the end, so to speak, or our outermost row. We'd switched things up at the last minute over the previous weekend, when we realised the ground was utterly too horrid to navigate with the tractor and tree planter in the planned parts. Instead, we worked different sides.

The planter had left a bare middle row and a bare innermost row along the north side of our field. I had already planted nineteen of the unwrapped trees, to prevent them from drying out, but Helen and I covered each half-mile side on foot, and planted almost two hundred of the extra trees by hand.

We tried to gauge if we were actually faster than the tree planter as we filled a twenty-tree long gap that was too rough for the machinery on the east side. Towards the south, we began planting the middle and innermost rows, and oh boy, what carnage lay before us as we found the results of Sunday's determined soldiering with no Quality Assurance department involved! For some stretches we had to replant every single tree.

One substantially-sized Siberian Crab Apple was actually completely upsidedown with its long sapling trunk buried and its rump of fine root hairs and potting soil pointing straight towards the sun. Many plants just lay exposed on the surface of the soil as though they had been tossed there with wanton abandon to wither at the hands of the elements.

Helen and I trudged row after row, backwards and forwards, turning a pleasant half-mile into a gruelling distance as we continued our quest. The cheese and bologna sandwiches we devoured late afternoon as a very postponed lunch never tasted so good. It felt great to have rescued all the oopsies. Now, finally, every tree was planted!

I had forgotten that I had promised dear friends a handful of our trees for their acreage. I was reminded by a phonecall that asked when our trees would be arriving so that they could choose some for themselves. I had my eldest son and grandson visiting, so we combined our outdoor wanderings with a bit of tree-removal, as I tried to explain to my two-year-old grandson that even though grandma was indeed digging up trees, this is not something he should ever do. It was a tricky lesson!

I was every bit as delighted to gift the small collection of saplings to my dear friends that were to receive them, even though I mentally kicked myself for not remembering and doubling my workload having already planted them (in some cases twice!) Jimmy then came home from a neighbour that he had gone to see, with a trailer load of maples, oak, and raspberry canes. Oh yay. He had bought us more trees!

***

Having tackled the weekend challenge of tree-planter and saplings, and having made a home for almost a hundred baby poultry that had both served to interrupt our hoop house building, it was time to get back to the hoop house. Foundations were set, with laminated lengths of two-by-six timber, laser-levelled and anchored throughout. We were going to need more pairs of hands to construct the steel frame and also to haul the double-skin polythene over the frame.

Would anyone even answer the phone if we called anymore? That tree planting was a bit of a doozy!

Inside our house, my seedlings were struggling still. I was losing peppers at quite a rate. Nestled at the very edge of the water blanket on the shelf, they were accumulating salt and minerals from the other soil blocks between them and the water source, that rose up like a huge crust, making the seedlings go brown and shrivel up.

The fenugreek that I had erroneously seeded early, because I didn't know any better, had already grown, flowered, formed pods, and had made a second generation of seeds… right there on the kitchen windowsill!

We had volunteered for a 'photovoice' research project with the University of Manitoba that spring, collecting and annotating photographs of our rollercoaster ride through organic and sustainable farming. One of the pictures I submitted was of Jimmy holding a tomato seedling that had been trapped in its two-inch soil block since February, and measured almost eighteen inches, on the thinnest and weakest stalk imaginable, as it spent its time reaching for that feeble window light.

We finished the hoop house frame by ourselves, with Jimmy and I doing our best through the day, and then Jimmy and the children carrying on into the evening hours. New projects and problems kept cropping up, and we finally decided the hoop house could wait. We were moments away from planting season anyway, and other things needed our attention.

One of those other things was the growing awareness that the tree saplings covering almost four linear miles had had no rain at all since they went into the ground a few weeks earlier. If we didn't do something soon, they would all die.

Whilst there are moments we are very grateful we have a large family and can muster up a significant amount of help, there are also moments when our children wish they were born to other parents, perhaps wealthy ones who took holidays to exciting destinations, or lazy ones who watched television and played video games all day. No doubt this was one of those moments for our children, when we announced we were going to spend the weekend watering all three thousand of our baby trees... by hand.

It took Jimmy four days to fill two of our 1000-litre totes from our well. (Our well is another 'problem' on our project list, by the way.) He loaded the totes onto a trailer, hooked the trailer to our truck, and off we went.

Each of us had a bucket and an old, empty 800ml tomato tin. One at a time, we filled our bucket from the tote, then carefully poured one tomato-tin of water onto each little sapling. Some of them were completely brown already, and likely doomed, but many of them had sprouted buds, and even leaves! It was a mix of sorrow and joy as we did the first lap of our farm.

It was gruelling and backache inducing, but also oddly meditational and peaceful. Our two younger sons couldn't catch-on to the peace and meditation aspect at all, however, and spent the whole time complaining and raging against God, Mother Nature, and all things outdoors.

Day two brought the other half of the job, and our eldest daughter once again volunteered her help to endure a day of hard graft. What a trooper! I offered our two younger sons an alternative opportunity of housework, which they not only agreed to, but also actually did a fantastic job! We returned from our arduous endeavours to find clean floors, tidy bedrooms, and clutter-free countertops! I have been thinking of a range of hideous manual labour tasks I can suggest, just so that I can garner a repeat performance from my boys as the 'alternative opportunity', but I am generally too soft for my own good. Alas, I am left to sweep my own floors… or not… as it turns out.

Still it seemed we had not yet had our fill of planting things!

I had persuaded Jimmy to visit a local Garden Centre by casually mentioning we could "just pop in there if we have time" during a city trip laden with other errands.

I had been to this Garden Centre the year before, taking my eldest son and his partner to collect a few perennials for their little garden at their rented property in town. I had just fallen in love with the place! I spent the winter months googling their website, feverishly reading details of all the plants offered, and making lists of the ones I wanted most that were hardy, productive, bee-friendly, scented or beautiful, or any combination of them all. I'd even transferred my list from my old diary of the previous year to my new diary of this year.

Jimmy had no idea what he was agreeing to when we pulled into their parking lot.

I began with onion sets, harmless enough and hardly worthy of the big trolley we'd pulled from the entrance. We also grabbed a few labels for my garden rows and took a quick look at larger house-plant pots for a future summer project.

Then, we entered the fruit tree section. Oh, what joy! We loaded an apple tree, a plum tree, and an apricot tree. I was reaching for the pear tree whilst scanning around for the cherry trees when Jimmy finally broke into a sweat, and said we had enough.

I still managed to drag him through the roses section, snagging four of my much-coveted rose bushes along the way, and "happening across" two juniper bushes, raspberry canes, and strawberry plants before reaching the checkout. I couldn't be sure, so ecstatic was I at my tremendous haul, but I think

Jimmy was whimpering.

One great mercy at spending such an enormous chunk of change in one go is that a person can be surprised by an unexpected discount. Jimmy conceded he should have let me take the pear tree and the cherry too with the discount they would have generated.

We planted the large fruit trees the next day.

Last year, we looked into Biodynamic Certification for our farm. It's more-or-less a step above organic certification, with a whole-systems level of sustainability, and a listening mind to climate, weather, moon phases, and cosmic influences from other planets. Off the cuff it can seem a bit hocus-pocus, but really it's just physics and microbiology.

The moon creates changes in gravitational pull on the earth. We know this if we watch the tides change. This pull affects plants a lot more than we might otherwise notice. Many dedicated souls have done all the grunt work in detailing these effects, and how a person might plan their plantings to use them to their best advantage.

We had bought and tried to follow a biodynamic planting calendar with varying degrees of success. It was good to put our trees in the ground on a particular day (a fruit day with a descending moon if you must know – now you definitely think I am a witch, don't you?)

An ice storm was forecast that week, and I had already taken a gamble and transplanted some of the more pathetic-looking tomato seedlings that were not thriving at all in their

'Richter's Pot Maker' paper pots. I chose to hold-off on my kitchen window leggy transplants. Whilst it was true they were slowly dying, slowly being the key word, an ice storm would surely finish them off overnight.

We used row cover to give the sad tomato seedlings the best chance we could, and we covered other small seedlings like the goji berries, hops, and little apple saplings with rubber feed tubs. We stashed the raspberries, strawberries, roses, and junipers in a shed.

It was almost three days later before the weather settled down enough to allow us to plant the raspberries, strawberries, roses, and junipers, not that they all got planted at once. I put two rose bushes into their Forever Home right in the middle of the vegetable garden, having read about the benefits of mixing-it-up with rotating annual food crops and perennials. I put the Never Alone beautiful red flowering rose bush to the west, and the Blanc de Coubert white one to the east.

The death of our calf, Moon (see Cowing section), meant both of my juniper bushes and two of my rose bushes got a hunk of slow-release fertilizer (aka cut-up calf remnants) under their root ball to give them a jumpstart into their new life on our farm. Being so close to the entrance of our home, I wanted the fragrant roses to have pride of place as corner sentries to my smaller herb garden.

The junipers are long-coveted low-ground-cover growing, and I set them both at the edge of the little patch directly in front of our house. Between the ground they will eventually cover and the expansion of the herb garden I have started, I plan to eliminate lawn altogether on this patch.

One of my older daughters once told me that lawn was invented by the aristocracy in Europe as a flagrant display of wealth. Only a rich person has the means to secure food from elsewhere, and does not need to grow food for themselves, unlike the lowly peasants. The presence of a lawn was evidence of such opulence.

Today, I feel a lawn is seen as 'normal', and second only to the vast expanse of concrete we eagerly smother our soil with. At least it photosynthesises I guess, going some way to tipping the scales back towards carbon-sequestering. With the fertilizers and weed-killing cocktails liberally applied by many, I can't think the tipping is enough.

We own and use a ride-on lawn mower, before I go too far down the path of soap-box preaching about all-things-environmental. We did decide to try mowing only pathways around most of our yard for the very first time this year. This year being what it turned out to be, mowing only happened once sometime in June. Heat, drought, and winds put some kind of hypnotic halt on grass-growing activities for the rest of the season.

Leaving swaths of 'wilderness patches' all over the place produced some interesting flowering plants and shrubs, and I can imagine a score of 'invisible' critters enjoying those spaces too.

The forecast ice storm that came through did not do any damage to the fruit trees, surprisingly. It tore great limbs from some of our trees in the yard, and encased branches and leaves in a sheet of ice that looked as though they were inside glass. It seems we chose a brilliant spot for the beginnings of our very own orchard.

In the main garden, our seedlings were so very slow to get started. Drought stress made the carrots refuse point blank to even peek out of the soil, and the parsnips and turnips were the same. The lettuces I direct-seeded did a little better. Squash seeds sprouted; my cereal seeds were excellent, and the seed-potatoes and onion sets looked great. I had thrown a full ziploc bag of rhubarb seeds, gifted to me by a dear friend back in Ontario, onto the ground and watered it with wavering regularity, with no discernable results.

The tomatoes, peppers, eggplants, and cabbage that I had nurtured for far too long in our kitchen window finally made it to the great outdoors. Some were so leggy I made a temporary 'wall' out of bits of timber to shield them from anything stronger than a light breeze.

Flower seeds, both purchased and stolen, were sown into the small herb garden at the front of our house, and these too stubbornly refused to participate in the prescribed growing program.

The weeks rolled on though, and little by little the miracle of life began to prevail. Glazing over the game of beat-the-gopher that began if we hoped to snag a strawberry from one of our new plants, and the digging-and-tunneling of one of the pesky little rodents that cost me at least four of my pepper plants that had survived the kitchen-window ordeal, it was fair to say the garden was looking good. Even those wimpy tomato seedlings in their paper pots had caught-up to their leggy siblings, and the tomato vines, scant as they were, were shaping up to be robust.

Then, in July, we got a 'plow wind' with hailstones. Nooooo…

Potato rows got thrashed, zucchini plants felled, and pole beans were stripped. Some of our neighbours got a worse dose. Bloody weather.

Helen visited one afternoon, and we set-off to walk the tree lines to see how our little saplings were getting on. My youngest daughter came with us. The outermost row showed that most of the White Spruce were doing well, with bright green new growth on the upper branches.

We had lost most of the Jack Pine, but the surviving ones looked fabulous with big branches of green tassels sprouting from the first spindly, feather-like twig we had planted. The middle row of Siberian Larch and Green Ash was fifty/fifty surviving/dead. The innermost row was the most pitiful. With all that variety, and what I had carefully selected as native species built to adapt to our mad prairie weather patterns, very few were showing any signs of life.

I had read an article somewhere that talked about the pampered nature of polystyrene-tube-grown saplings versus the survival-of-the-fittest hardiness of natural tree growth localised around parent trees. Maybe it was too much to expect. Still, never one to be thwarted by such a detail as glaring and dismal failure, I had made my order for the next spring, another three-thousand-or-so saplings.

PART 5

Beeing

Sent on a mission to pick up the latest batch of bee
supplies, my dear friend Helen and I met in our local
town of Lumsden. She rode in on her motorbike
from the city, and I took our truck the short distance down
the highway to meet her. The bike remained parked in her
nephew's driveway while we made the three-and-a-half hour
road trip north to the BeeMaid store.

Helen is an enthusiastic environmentalist, known for picking
up bottles and cans from the roadside while she pedal-bikes
her way to and from substitute teacher jobs. She introduced
me to the concept of pee cloths (like washable sanitary pads

or cloth diapers, but really small and simple) which we were eternally grateful for when the pandemic first hit and every wally and his wife bought up all the bathroom tissue instead of acting like responsible, kind citizens and taking only what they needed.

Helen even undertakes green investment, choosing to use her money to support organizations or groups from which she may never see any personal return herself, like solar co-ops. She is stellar, but it meant there was a slim-to-zero chance of slipping in a much coveted meal stop at A&W. No. We would be taking our own supplies with us.

Helen made snacks of raw vegetables, fruit, home-made crackers and cheese pieces. I prepared two hot coffee-mochas in to-go cups, two juice and water cocktails in to-go cups, and two plain water bottles using steel bottles with screw-lids and carabiners. I gifted one of these to Helen and painted her name with what the limits of my artistic prowess could pass-off as a 'fancy design'. I also made two hot lunches in the little squat, wide-mouth thermos flasks that you can eat out of. It was spaghetti bolognese with extra rosemary-garlic fried potatoes on top.

The first hour was rather fun. There we both were, swilling down hot chocolate and coffee, decadently loaded with cream from our own Jersey cow. We were Thelma and Louise for sure, although Helen isn't very keen on Brad Pitt. I couldn't imagine Brad ambling along the side of a deserted Saskatchewan highway anyway, so I didn't think we needed to fight about it.

The second hour was also fun, but a distinct feeling of "Are we there yet?" was setting in. I love Saskatchewan, so much that when we left it to go spend two and a half years in Ontario, I wanted to come back. Coming from almost forty years of life in England, with traffic jams, road rage, and edge-of-the-seat hairpin bends all over the place, I still find those endless stretches of deserted Saskatchewan highway just adorable!

Helen was itching to pick up the bottles and cans she could spy in the ditch as we travelled along. At more than one point I thought she might try to insist I stop and let her hop out to gather a few that were clustered together. I could imagine her with a big fishing-net sort of thing, trawling along the ditches through her passenger side window, snagging every bit of detritus out there with glee. It may have been my imagination, but I'm sure some of the time, she actually sat on her hands.

We got to the BeeMaid store, and the two folks managing the place were happy to see us and load up the pallet they had prepared with Jimmy's order.

Jimmy had requested that they help strap the load down in the back of the truck. It's not that I can't successfully strap anything down, and certainly Helen can, the world traveller that she is. Often armed with only her motorbike and her tent on many occasions, she can haul any item necessary in panniers or on a rack. But Jimmy secretly worries (not very secretly, of course, which is how I know about it) that I'll goof up royally, and we'll spend the three and a half hours journeying home littering those lonely Saskatchewan highways with a range of beehive frames and boxes, while blithely pressing the accelerator and gossiping without pause or a passing glance in the rear view mirror.

I wouldn't do this. I was a Girl Guide! In fact, in 1985 I was awarded the rather prestigious Queen's Guide Award. It is not to be confused with the Duke of Edinburgh Award, which is actually really hard, apparently involving something comparable to a Decathlon or Olympic Sport in addition to University Challenge problem-solving and Map Quest missions that would baffle a SWAT team.

My Queen's Guide Award involved gathering an armful of badges, each one awarded when I reached a level of competence in a skill that appeased the appointed (volunteer) tester; things like cooking on an outdoor fire, map reading (at a lesser level than a SWAT team's), pitching and striking a ridge-pole tent, tidying my bedroom, that sort of thing.

Alongside the badges were separate challenges like community volunteering (mine was a whole summer in a lovely old folks home a bike-ride away from my Burntwood home town in the West Midlands of England), attending camps, and helping other Guides or Brownies get their badges.

I was a wizard at camping and lighting my fire in the pouring rain. I learned very quickly that if you munch on stolen cookies in your sleeping bag, an ants' nest will move right in before you wake up. I could handle latrine duty and became adept at building "gadgets", things that you use to keep your bedding rolls off the damp ground, or to balance your washing-up bowl in with a drying rack to one side for doing dishes.

But nowhere did I ever strap down a load of beehives onto a trailer.

I still think Jimmy could have had a bit more confidence in me, but Jimmy has also learned the hard way to extend a bit of caution to some situations where his slightly-distracted and over-optimistic wife is concerned.

In the BeeMaid store, I spotted the candle-making equipment. I'd done a bit of reading and was pretty confident I could give this a go. I had been making my own furniture polish (roughly equal quantities of beeswax and oil, then around half the quantity – if that – of natural turpentine) for a few years. I could tackle candles!

In listing our honey, out of sheer desperation, on FB Marketplace a couple of months earlier (my advice in consequence to this is do not list your honey, or anything else frankly, on FB Marketplace!), I'd had a lady interested in buying our beeswax. I'd kept all of it and tried several different methods of getting the honey and bits of dead bee out of it.

Over the years, Jimmy had kept bees. It wasn't the first time I'd been approached by someone wanting beeswax. Jimmy prices our honey at a dollar-amount-per-pound, plus the cost of the jar, which annoyingly we have to buy new every time, according to Public Health. We have some customers who bring their washed jar back to us, but that is a private sale, what you might call 'Farm Gate', which Public Health is less interested in.

Pricing beeswax was a new game, and I had no idea how to play it. A bit of Googling revealed that beeswax can-and-should cost many times more than the honey, because there is so little of it comparatively, and there is far more work involved to separate it from residual honey and bits of dead bee.

I took a wild stab-in-the-dark and used a price similar to something from far-off lands (that might not have been real beeswax considering the documentaries I've encountered recently that tell us it's not even real honey folks buy from the store half the time) listed on an online store. My Interested Lady was delighted, which suggests I underpriced myself by a lot.

I went to all the trouble of weighing the pieces I had, as accurately as was possible with my inherited-for-free kitchen scale, wrapping them separately, and arranging a pick-up date which would involve me staying home-and-available at the allotted time. She was a no-show. And this was the theme we found in general with our online FB Marketplace presence. We wasted a whole bunch of time messaging back-and-forth with folks who wanted honey to be dropped-off even though we don't offer a delivery service.

We once foolishly agreed to drop-off our honey jars to folks in the city, when we were there running other errands. One guy I met bartered me down by a significant amount, and being the wimp I am in confrontational situations, I let him. He wanted to be a repeat customer, but got Jimmy on his second round, who would not budge an inch from our designated price. (Yay, Jimmy!) This guy had no idea the work involved in making honey!

When he complained that the correct price was too expensive, Jimmy simply put the jars back in the box and said, "Okay then." Our customer was pretty speedy producing the right amount of cash when he realized Jimmy was not the wimp I was!

Waiting for no-shows, bartering for a fair and already-stated price, and spending too many hours juggling dead-end messages led to me removing our post. I had committed to two local farmers' markets, only one of which would allow me to sell our honey (the other having too many honey vendors already), and I decided this was the better way to go.

With that thought in mind, I had high hopes-and-dreams of not just honey, but gift baskets, to go with gift-giving seasonal occasions like Christmas, Mother's Day, Father's Day, and doesn't someone have a birthday pretty much every day of the year?

I have made beeswax wraps in the past, a bit of a fail if I'm honest, but I gave it a shot with Christmas gifts for my grown children given I try hard not to do the let's-buy-stuff-we-don't-want-or-need-for-each-other thing. I used beeswax, pine resin, and jojoba oil, but I used the combined 'glue' too sparingly. The fabric wouldn't stick to itself very well… it needed more chewing-gum-ness.

If I could master the beeswax food wraps, and make a dazzling candle or two, throw in a jar of honey, or better yet, some Comb Honey, what a gift basket that would be!

So I am standing in the BeeMaid store, the pallet of Jimmy's hive things are loaded (and strapped down) already. I am there to look at something called 'Ross Rounds'. This is a way of making Comb Honey that doesn't require cutting through the regular honey comb, making it drip and ooze all over the place. The rounds are set right into the beehive, and the bees work with the shape (apparently), making something that looks like a round of the French cheese called 'Brie'. The box calls it a 'Complete Ross Rounds Kit', and it is not until I get all the way home again and look at it the next day that it becomes obvious this is a lie.

But in the meantime, there I am. I'm going to buy the Ross Rounds Kit of course. I cannot imagine how just looking at the round reusable plastic circles is going to infuse me with any wisdom at all on actually producing Comb Honey. I've bought a book for that (and a book on candle making too!), which I notice is a duplicate of the copy provided free with the Ross Rounds kit. Do I challenge the delightful staff at the BeeMaid store and demand my money back on the book I just paid for? I think I've already mentioned how non-confrontational I am, so that was a "no". He had strapped that pallet on for me after all!

We threw the 'Complete Ross Rounds Kit' into the truck, and my attention was drawn to the candle making section. I had promised myself I wouldn't actually buy anything until I'd finished reading the book I'd bought, which was in the truck alongside the bought-and-paid-for Comb Honey book (identical to the free Comb Honey book with the Ross

Rounds Kit).

But we had just driven three and a half hours to get here. I wasn't in a hurry to come again, and there would be postage and packing to pay for if I ordered at a later date online, right? I was right there, in the store, looking at the candle moulds, the wicks, the mould release spray…

I bought a silicone mould of a bear climbing over a beehive. It's a bit cheesy, but they had sold-out of the beehive-by-itself mould. I bought a mile (or something) of the recommended wick size, and I totally forgot the mould release spray. (There's a whole other story set in 'Michael's' that involves an hour-long line up only to find the last, sad bottle of mould release spray they had that I could slide in here, but it seems cruel.)

Helen and I were loaded-up and now headed home!

Chappy-bod at the store had suggested we stop after a few miles and check the tension of our strapping. (Were we qualified for this?) We did and it was as loose as a Lady of the Night's knickers, flapping around behind us like some kind of flag. I couldn't see this in my mirror; it was on Helen's side. It took a while to notice because Helen, not being the driver, was not checking her mirror as frequently as I was checking mine.

We pulled over at the front of a homestead, miles from any other homestead, or anything else at all. Helen couldn't help herself and hunted up a couple of bottles in the ditch to throw into the truck. Then, we worked together to tighten the strapping. We are not stupid women. Helen has two degrees, and all told I have four, but do you think we could figure out the release trigger on that strap? Jimmy was right! It's a science beyond my boundaries!

We heaved and we tugged. We released a few paltry inches and squeezed it over by hand to try and capture some purchase on a corner. Images of strewn frames and boxes bounded through my head. I will certainly goof up royally here. Helen grabbed one more bottle she spotted in the ditch, and we headed off once again.

The miles passed, and the straps seemed oddly to be holding. We chatted about life, the universe, and everything. I am not the best driver in the world, but I like to think I'm not terrible. I notice things. We passed a police car heading the other way to us, and I noticed right away that he turned his flashing lights on, made a U-turn, and came up behind us. I said outloud to Helen, "Huh, look there's a police car with its lights on, turning around and following us."

I began to pull over almost on autopilot. With most of my driving years based in the busy traffic of England, I had always understood that if you see flashing lights, or hear a siren, you should just get out of the way and turn the nose of your car curbside. There are folks who will try to outrun the emergency vehicle, gun-it and get past, but my aversion to adrenaline dictates I just slowly, carefully, and safely get out of the way!

Helen said he probably got an emergency call, had to turn around and is now chasing down some hideous perpetrator of crime. I felt rather foolish with my getting-out-of-the-way strategy being employed on a deserted Saskatchewan highway with no other traffic in sight. Perhaps I shouldn't have been surprised when those flashing lights parked themselves right behind our truck, or when Mr. Uniform casually left his vehicle and approached mine, but I was. I really was.

My family tease me for being a 'snail driver'. One time here on our new farm, Jimmy and our son were in the field when I was arriving home, and our son asked, "Why does Mum slow down so much to turn into the driveway?" And Jimmy told him, "She's not turning in; she's been driving that slow the whole time."

This was the first time ever, in my whole fifty years of living, that I've been pulled over by the police. Not a fan of the adrenaline now coursing through my veins, and totally a non-confrontational person, I began to shake like a leaf. I looked at Helen in a panicked way that spoke volumes of normal, functional abilities lost, and asked her what I should do. She explained the drill of rolling your window down, not getting out of the vehicle, and communicating with the officer, in any language other than gibberish.

What if I got out of the vehicle by mistake? What if I forgot which language I spoke, or forgot I could even speak at all? What if I rolled the wrong window down? (Oh Jimmy, I wish I'd paid more attention when you were blathering on about all those switches!)

What if I pressed the horn, you know, in one of those moments where you do the thing you totally shouldn't do, but it overwhelms you and you do it anyway? What if we actually arc Thelma and Louise? I could speed off as he strides powerfully back to his kit-car-of-all-things-fine-related. We could drive off a… well not cliff, not here in the prairies… how about a shallow ditch? Or a small patch of brush or scrub? Less a suicide pact, more a bald tire. And Mr. Uniform would probably be in hot pursuit on foot.

So I sat still. I rolled the correct window down (thank you, Jesus) and smiled. Well I think it was a smile. It may have looked to Mr. Uniform like the guffaw of a deranged madwoman; I don't know.

He started up our conversation with pleasantries. It made me wonder if I was actually being pulled over or whether he just felt a little bored and wanted to test out his lights and sirens! "How're you today? Where're you headed?" Oh thank the Lord, he just wants a nice little chat… phew!

I'm still shaking, but I manage to waffle through the fact that we just drove out to where-was-it to collect hives, yes, beehives, for my husband you see, and we're just taking them home to him (we're not Thelma and Louise at all, we are very sensible gals actually…) Where is home? Well, it's Lumsden, well not really Lumsden itself you see, we're on a farm… blah blah blah…

He asked for license and registration. Well, I can find my license, right here in my purse, no problem! Registration documents? Ahh, give me a minute. I know they'll be in here somewhere.

Some years ago when we lived on our Kelliher farm, Jimmy showed me where he kept the registration documents for our vehicle. At the time, I didn't know why he was showing me, but I recall it was in the elastic of one of the pull-down visor-things above the driver's or passenger's seat. The sort of visor you can use to block the sun, or find a drop-down mirror to apply some form of cosmetic paste to yourself if you are that way inclined. That's all I had in my head; some sort of drop-down visor was secreting the documents I sought.

Helen and I went through that truck, nerves-a-jangling like a real Thelma and Louise situation, but without the ultimate get-out clause, looking for drop-down anything. Helen starts hunting through the central console, which is a catch-all for any piece of crap and detritus imaginable. Mr. Uniform is getting impatient and tells me that while he is willing to let me off my speeding ticket, he had clocked me at 120 km/hr while my speedometer showed only 110, but as he rightfully reminded me, we were actually in a 100 km/hr zone, so "whatever". He is keen to let me off with just a warning for my speeding, but will ding me for failure to find my registration documents.

Intently dealing with whatever computer system is installed in police vehicles these days, (and I've no doubt it is extensive… probably takes over the whole car, but perhaps the lonely Saskatchewan highway patrol guys can at least watch Netflix on it between bored-and-slightly-speeding patrons?) Mr. Uniform is back in his vehicle, when Helen finally finds the registration documents in the cluttered console.

"Wag them out of the window!" she instructs. "Or maybe do get out of the car, and show him we found them!" Well, I've seen 'Meet the Parents'. I'm not going to be that guy, tazered to the vehicle by an anal policeman, though he's in no mood to look up. That computer gizmo is all-consuming. Seems like ticket printing is the new vogue.

With a sigh I put my too-late registration documents away, and figure perhaps our local constabulary is hoping for an early Christmas bonus this year.

The fine for not producing the registration documents was one hundred dollars. Jimmy was incensed! He phoned the legal folks to see if he could do anything, since we had the documents, and produced them for Mr. Uniform, just not in the timeframe he had hoped for. He was told we could show up in court and contest. He asked if we actually had to show up. Could we not make a phone call? Well, in the first instance, yes, a phone call would work, but once the "trial" or whatever it was called, rolled around, we would have to show up. It would cost us more in gas to get there than the fine was for. We paid the fine.

***

I developed a poorly-placed confidence, despite my menopausal-related anxiety issues, in walking through the bee yard this year. Our bee hives grew spectacularly from the four winter-survivors to a heady nine after Jimmy bought two new 'nucs' (small nucleus colonies), split two hives, and captured an early July swarm.

I had spent the winter months and much of the previous autumn trying to grow hops from seed, which is a super tricky affair. They need a six month cold-stratification period followed by a three-to-twelve-month cold growing period, all of which I accomplished.

Hops are fabulous in my opinion. Not only is it one of the key ingredients in making beer, but also a medicinal remedy for bees fighting the good fight against the Varroa Mite, a nasty parasite responsible for decimating more of our beloved and necessary buzzing pollinators than is fair. I had grown hop plants (transplants, not from seed), when we lived on our farm at Kelliher, some years before. They thrived year-after-year, despite our Saskatchewan winters. I even harvested a large bag of flower heads, determined to brew my own beer with them, but chose to abandon them to the compost heap after some years of toting them around, because my first attempt at homemade beer resulted in a brew that tasted like vomit. I couldn't muster the resolve or courage to try the process again despite lying to myself that I eventually would.

The ordeal of growing hops from seed was somewhat successful, and the resulting survivors were tended-to with due diligence given the difficulty of their inception.

In addition to hops, was amaranth. It was also something I'd grown before, and witnessed the lofty height and spectacular blossom it yields.

Both of these were for the bees' benefit, and planted in places that were close to the bee yard.

On this particular day, I wanted to water the inconvenient-for-me-but-such-a-gift-for-the-bees hops and amaranth seedlings, that frankly were really struggling with the current weather conditions of hot and dry.

I am sensible enough, even after a few glasses of wine, to give the beehives a wide berth. I understand the need for quiet confidence and respect when walking near the hives; the only time I got stung recently was because a little bee was perched on a clothes peg as I was taking in line-dried laundry. I didn't see her and my hand closed in over the peg… bang!

She stung me (and died, as is the unfortunate consequence for a bee when it feels compelled to sting). At the time, I wasn't even sure it was a bee sting. Within a few hours it itched and itched, and I wondered if it was a horse-fly bite, and not a bee sting.

I had filled my watering can with rainwater we had harvested in old food-grade IBC totes, (1000 litre plastic containers in a metal cage for reinforcement that have an exit valve at their base) and stole my way through the low-hanging caragana trees that we deliberately installed our beehives under for shade and east-facing warmth. Preceding this manoeuvre, and temporarily blocking my common sense, was an early-morning sprinkler on that was set to water the herb garden for twenty minutes or so, that I tried to time, dodge, and weave past.

I'm not sure why I thought it would be fine, but I did. I decided to creep behind the first cluster of four hives, two facing forward, two facing back, where I would normally walk wide-and-around. Perhaps it was a way to avoid the sprinkler or perhaps a temporary leave of my senses. In any case, my can and I strode too close to the hive exit. It was less than a second before a small cluster of bees, two or maybe three, gathered on the calf of my left leg to begin their "Bugger

Off!" attack.

At the time, I couldn't tell if it was one sting or a thousand. The pain was instant and searing. My watering can dropped. I hobbled, replete with invectives, back towards the house, mercifully only a few yards away.

I sat at the kitchen table, and Jimmy took out his pen-knife. There was one stinger (What? Just one?) hanging out of my calf, along with the intestines of the kamikaze bee that chose to administer it. The best way to remove a stinger is to scrape carefully and thoroughly with a knife blade.

Oh the agony! I was all-a-jitter, and could barely breathe. (What a wus.)

It was utterly necessary that I rest (ahem), even when Helen showed up having ridden the better part of an hour on her Shadow to come and help with weeding for the third time that season. Well, I got over myself, went outside and gave the garden fury with Helen, and almost forgot about the assault. That is until "The Itch" moved in. That little sting on the hand that had happened when I gathered laundry in was not a horsefly bite after all. It seems there is an itch to a vicious and painful bee sting… and, oh boy, is it an ITCH!

My leg swelled a little, not too much, but a day of Farmers' Market standing was enough to send those histamine hormones wild and create a hot, hard, red patch of itch the size of a tea-plate. It stood to deprive me of sleep for at least two nights.

I was monastic in my determination not to scratch; I could

probably have removed my entire calf muscle with nothing other than my clipped-short fingernails had I given-in to the urge to scratch (clear and indisputable evidence of self-control beyond the sphere of drinking wine).

Two sleepless nights was a fair estimate, despite taking antihistamines and a Tylenol or two. I cast my lure frequently for sympathy from my family, with no joy at all. I hadn't swollen up to the extent of Jimmy the time he got multiple stings on one hand that looked like manicured elephantiasis, which we photographed for posterity. No, I was just me with an itchy leg.

The leg then started turning purple, and once again I was the only one who seemed remotely alarmed by this. More worrying was "The Itch", which radiated out from the purple and invaded surrounding calf tissue, shin, ankle, and ultimately foot, invisibly and without remorse. Then, blisters, tiny little blisters, began radiating from the sting site. Oh no! My leg could very well explode!

Ultimately, it took days, almost a week, with discolouration and discomfort before showing signs of letting up. Jimmy said, "Are you allergic? Do I have to get rid of the bees?" And while I was formulating my answer, "No, of course not darling," he added, "I don't want to get rid of them, you know." I recognised instantly my place in the hierarchy of All Things; the bees will win, and rightly so.

The next time I got stung, I had been escorting a local artist who had worked miracles on our small Farmers' Market trailer back to our house, after taking a look at her completed and very impressive work. Nowhere near the hives at all, I felt a quick stab on the back of my right hand. Dang! I knew what it was, and I knew what would probably happen next.

The next morning my hand looked like it was ready to explode. It almost formed a sphere, such was the swelling! I could barely make my fingers co-operate with the signals from my brain, and simple tasks like eating, writing, or unbuttoning my trousers were a massive challenge. "The Itch" cost me two more nights' sleep, and no amount of antihistamine seemed to have any effect. "The Itch" moved around, just as before, spreading up my arm, past my wrist. Small blisters followed.

Once again, Jimmy gazed upon my pitiful state, and said he thought I was definitely allergic. Did he really have to get rid of the bees? I knew the script of course, "No darling, not at all!" I can just pray I never get stung near my airway.

***

The truck-load of hive equipment was rapidly put to use, as Jimmy added box upon box to the active hives. Towards the end of summer, it looked like one of the 'nucs' he had bought had amounted to nothing, and we lost a hive, bringing us down to eight. Perhaps the Queen excluder hadn't worked? Perhaps the colony had failed? If I could speak 'Bee', I'd ask them.

Conversely, my solitary candle mould was still in the packaging. Following the FB Marketplace no-show, I had a couple more interested parties in our beeswax, so I chose to blame my cowardly procrastination on them. But the truth was I needed to take a leap of faith in giving this enterprise a go. Feeling overwhelmed with so many other aspects of our new farming endeavours, I was just ignoring this avenue.

As the end of the season approached, and Jimmy had extracted enough honey to service our Farmers' Market and a bunch of Farm-Gate buyers (folks who purchase from us directly), I felt the appropriate level of shame for my inactivity with the candle bit. The Ross Rounds were looking suspect. It seemed as though the bees didn't know what to do with the strangely-shaped plastic contraptions. Time would tell if they would materialize into the fabulous components of a gift basket we were hoping for or not.

But the adventure is never over! The winter months may bring a "hive" (tee hee!) of activity. And may God Bless the bees!

PART 6

Abouting

I wouldn't really consider myself a traveller. There are folks I know who yearn to travel the world, or who have travelled the world. I've just never been one of those people. My yearning was always for family.

I remember telling my horrified mother when I was something like nineteen years old that I really wanted to have a baby. I actually had my first baby at twenty-two, and I went on to have more babies right up until I was thirty nine, not consistently mind you. I was married for a first time and then married for a second time (to Jimmy) that included the three children from my first marriage.

Jimmy and I lost our first baby; a little girl who grew inside me for seventeen weeks before she simply stopped. Even a post-mortem after her delivery did not reveal why; I suppose sometimes these things just happen.

Of eight births, I have seven living children.

Travel was something other people did, and yet it seemed to become a part of my story almost as an add-on. I grew up in the West Midlands of England. I had a thick Brummie accent for thirteen years until my parents moved to another county and the teasing at school forced me to adopt a more rounded, non-specific dialect (though I can still produce a pretty decent Brum when requested!)

Some years of my childhood included summers spent in the north of France – Brittany and Normandy – both incredibly beautiful places! I loved the language and did well at it in high school. As a teenager I travelled with buddies around Holland, picked up a little Dutch and thoroughly enjoyed the culture. I also studied German, and got to visit Bavaria in my twenties to house-sit for relatives. One year Jimmy and I outdid ourselves when we decided to visit his sister in Malawi. That was a phenomenal experience! But still, I did not think I was a traveller.

I moved around a lot in my adult years, with around thirty different addresses in England if I included all my student digs. When we landed in Saskatchewan in 2007, I figured it was time to put down some roots at long last, and actually call the place Home.

Home was a fair-sized farm, a very large-scale farm in UK

terms, with ten "quarter sections" (each quarter section is 160 acres). I think the labelling "quarter" is from when land was originally (and erroneously, now that we support the Truth and Reconciliation Commission and accept all the atrocities committed by the early western settlers) divided into square plots for sale that were one-mile-by-one-mile denoting one section. I guess at some point those sections got divided into four equal, smaller squares, that were a-half-mile-by-a-half-mile or a quarter mile squared. It all seems logical really, if a little befuddling to my English brain.

I worked hard to put down roots on our beautiful piece of the world near the small town of Kelliher, Saskatchewan, but being a foreigner to the Prairies, I was as ignorant as they came. I had outrageous fantasies about growing Christmas trees, wild flowers, or raising elk.

Jimmy was by himself for a couple of months right at the beginning, as I had to return to England to sell our old house (a beautiful brick Victorian terrace which we had spent the short time of our ownership restoring and renovating to a phenomenal standard), pack-up our prized possessions for shipping, and say goodbye to everything else. Everything else included not only my sister, my parents and my nieces, but also my three oldest children, who at the time were eleven, thirteen, and fourteen years old.

It was an incredibly painful chapter of my life and theirs, and with the benefit of hindsight, I would have fought tirelessly for a very different outcome. Still, with the back-and-forth that began our lives there and continued for several years, it was Jimmy who ultimately decided the fate of our first

Canadian farm. We went with conventional grain farming in the style of our predecessors.

Our youngest two children were born after we immigrated; a couple of true Canadians!

I was tasked with driving the grain truck, a feisty old thing we had bought second-hand from a nearby dealer. It had no synchro-mesh gear box, and while I never really understood what that means, I did learn very quickly that I needed to press the rather stiff clutch pedal twice before I could change gears. It was better than a Stairmaster for building thigh muscle, just such a shame it was only the one thigh!

With an impressive brood of babies, toddlers, and pre-schoolers still at-heel, I made a sort of lounging-sofa-thing that would nest between the passenger seat of the truck and the driver's seat. There was a fair distance between the two with only a large and unwieldy gear stick to navigate around. The arrangement worked quite well as we continued to work harvest hours that went well into the night.

Being afraid of the dark, or more specifically afraid of the outside dark and all the critters lurking beyond the perimeter of my night vision, I did not enjoy getting out of the coziness of my cab to start up the tractor, engage the auger, and begin the noisy process of transferring grain, but I had to get used to it. Being the truck driver meant I returned to our yard every time my truck was full, to tip the load into one of our grain bins using the tractor-powered auger.

During this time, I could sprint to the house and warm food for hungry children (hungry grown-ups too!), grab a couple more clean diapers, (and I should add we were using washable cloth diapers here), and sprint back to the truck before both the load had finished tipping or any of the babies had woken up.

Jimmy would accommodate a short person in the cab of his combine-harvester too. We would alternate the baby in the car-seat having nap-time in the continuously rocking combine-harvester and returning to mum for breastfeeding while sitting stationary in the truck, with inquisitive toddlers and their snacks and drinks. It was really not fun at all. There had to be a better way!

I had spent a couple of years before we left England training and qualifying to be a college lecturer. After our Canadian babies were old enough to join kindergarten or nursery school, I decided to try and adapt my qualification to work in the local grade school of our small town. The hours would work for the children which by now included the youngest of my first three children, who had come to join us from England, and would soon include my eldest daughter, who would successfully accomplish both her Canadian high school diploma and the remainder of her English General Certificates of Secondary Education (GCSEs) in tandem.

It didn't take much to bridge the educational gap and before long I was working a series of temporary contracts as a substitute teacher in two of our nearest towns. I wasn't completely off the hook with those grain fields though. After a day of battle in the hallways and classrooms, I did a second shift as cook and delivery service for the team that frequently helped us out in the fields, since my work became off-farm.

I would pack up to a dozen hot meals in separate insulated lunch kits, with drinks and desserts, and drive out to each combine, grain truck, tractor, swather, or whatever else piece of machinery was being manned, promptly delivering hot and hearty meals to the working folks out there.

Our team became very large because the wonderful farmers in our neighbourhood developed a sort of cooperative, working through all of their farms in turn, but as one unit. Each of the wives or off-farm workers took their turn at meal delivery when the team moved to their farm. It was genius while it lasted!

There are good years and bad years with grain farming. Some folks can buffer the bad years with help from family, or an inheritance that reduces the ongoing debt. We had neither of those things, and our third bad year turned out to be the one that ruined us. It is the only time I have ever seen Jimmy heartbroken since the day we left the hospital with the news that our first baby was no longer alive and would need to be born abortively within 48 hours.

We had already sold half of the land we first bought to get to that third year, and now we needed to auction off all of our machinery and think of something else. Jimmy took farm work jobs for other big operations in the area, and I took every teaching contract going. I bought half a dozen pigs from one neighbour, and a pair of orphan lambs from another. A small herd of goats followed, and finally our first pair of dairy cows.

Well, this was more like it! We had an eclectic mix of

livestock and we had begun growing vegetables and herbs. I wanted to extend the yard area we used to bring some draft horses into the mix, and the local tree-growing service provided almost four thousand trees for me to do so. One of my wonderful friends (my "sis") had moved her whole family to Canada on the back of a visit to us in our earlier years. Although they didn't stay in Canada, we both still recall fond memories of their time here, including their amazing efforts with the tree planter when I decided to put a small forest into our Kelliher soil!

The draft horse dream did not become reality despite my very best efforts in horse and horse-equipment acquisition; I learned that the fear of things-bigger-than-me, sparked in the early years of my time on Jimmy's home farm back in England, had not faded one jot. I felt rather defeated as I simply offered to contribute to the cost of feed and care for the two Clydesdales I had bought, but not taken from their home farm.

A new chapter in our lives opened as we became a foster family, and over the course of two and a half years, we took in nine little souls for varying lengths of time. Whether it was burn-out from fostering, or whether the politics and challenges of mainstream school finally overwhelmed me, or whether it was an unseen flood of perimenopausal hormones (and with the benefit of hindsight, I strongly suspect the latter), "Home" suddenly didn't feel like home anymore. My feet were itching; I was looking for something else.

The wretchedness I had often experienced with fostering and teaching (most especially in my frequent contracts as a

Learning Supports teacher) led me to a course of study in Anthroposophy, which took two years to complete and gain my certification with the Rudolf Steiner Centre in Toronto. It was an intense philosophy that seemed to illuminate areas of my evolving faith journey that challenged me, and served to heighten my belief in a better model of education than I had seen so far.

The Something Else manifested itself in a job vacancy I found online at a Waldorf Steiner school in Ontario. I sent in my application and was delighted to hear I had been invited for an interview! I even travelled all the way into Regina to my eldest daughter's residence, a two hour trip from our farm at that time, chauffeured by one extremely generous friend, to be sure I had a good internet connection for the virtual meeting.

The job involved a 75% pay cut from my regular teacher's salary, but I was so convinced of the merits beyond pay that this position would bring, I accepted the position despite many warnings from friends and loved ones, even my Anthroposophy tutor, that I was jumping too fast.

Jimmy was at a loss. Should we sell our farm? We'd put ten years into the place, with some phenomenal renovations on top of all those marvelous trees. We loved our little town, and all our wonderful friends there. Did we really want to just leave? But I was full steam ahead and not listening to anyone.

We planned our route, with a view to travelling Beverly-Hill-Billy style across three provinces, stopping for sleepovers at pre-booked stops.

What follows are some of the original emails I wrote on that trip, keeping my family in England and my three older children I was leaving (once again) behind, informed of our progress.

We set off on New Year's Eve, an odd time to want to begin such a long journey, but I had an early January start date for my new job, and we pretty much thought, "Why not?"

HEADING EAST

December 29, 2016

Hello!

Just a quick update to put you all in the loop of our imminent excursion:

We've added a day to our trip. A guy who bought some of our farm machinery at the auction sale has offered to put us up for the night in Manitoba on New Year's Eve.

It will cut a couple of hours off our Day Two drive (which formerly looked like twelve and a half hours not including any stops... Yikes!)

So, our route is Manitoba, stopping just east of Winnipeg; then on to Thunder Bay in Ontario for our second night; then over to New Liskeard, in Ontario (near Quebec border), for our third night; and then travel south to Durham, hopefully arriving afternoon/

supper time.

I'll let you know when we "land"!

Loads of love,

Jo xxxxxxxxx

The friends who so graciously accommodated us in Manitoba were phenomenal. It was New Year's Eve, and they had arrangements to be elsewhere for the timely celebrations. But no effort was spared to organise a bedroom for our girls, a bedroom for our boys, and a bedroom for us. A supper was laid out for us, and a full breakfast the next morning. I am still awed by the efforts these folks went to, who, quite frankly, hardly knew us! We still keep in touch, albeit infrequently.

On we trundled, eastward-bound. Each driving stint was between ten and fourteen hours with only essential bathroom breaks thrown in. We were driving an old fifteen-seater minibus that we bought back in our Foster Family days, to accommodate the many, many children we were often transporting. It was filled to capacity with "stuff" and, of course, children.

A dear friend and teaching colleague from Kelliher had gifted us the treasure of snacks, drinks, and entertainment in the form of colouring and reading books, a fantastic cache that got us through the bulk of those intense on-the-road days. The bus was towing our 'Fast Toys For Boys' trailer, which we bought from the previous owners of our Kelliher farm. Its former purpose was the transportation of bedding plants to and from the on-farm greenhouse at the time.

We had been careful to pack just the essentials for our interim rental in Durham Town, including a fully-stocked chest freezer that received the benefit of being plugged-in at each of our overnight stops. The food in there would last us for a few months at least. We'd bought a couple of chests-of-drawers, each drawer packed to accommodate more than one season's worth of clothes for our four youngest children and myself. If I put my packing-and-planning skills on my C.V., I wonder if NASA would be interested in recruiting my services for the next space mission...

January 1, 2017

Hello Family!

I am writing from our Super 8 motel room in Thunder Bay, at 9pm local time.

We made it this far!

We have totalled 1300 km, doing 900 of them today (and just over 400 yesterday). This leaves us just over 900 km tomorrow, and then only about 500 km on our last leg.

I did a measly two-hour shift of driving, between Kenora (Ontario) and Ignace. Jim, bless him, has done all the rest. (My Hero!)

We left the very hospitable Manitoba home at 7:30

this morning only stopping for a total of 2 hours, taking bathroom breaks, fueling, and eating lunch. We gained an hour crossing the time zone at Thunder Bay, so our 12 hour journey suddenly became 13. But only with about 10 hours of actual driving... not bad!

If you thought Saskatchewan landscape held a whole lot of nothing... you should see Manitoba! We all got quite excited when we crossed the "mid-Canadian longitude line"... marked by a solitary road-sign... that gives you a clue of the general level of interesting surroundings!

Ontario landscape is infinitely better, with thick forest, rocks, and winding roads... but after nine hours of that, it too seemed rather dull... No bloody pleasing some people, eh?

Having not really moved (stuck in a vehicle) for a day and a half, we can't decide if we are hungry or not, tired or not, and the children seem to just want to run around the hotel room and bounce on the beds.

Just two more days...

Will check-in with you all at tomorrow evening's landing! Happy 2017!

Mum/Jo, & Jim, & very antsy children xxxxxx

Thunder Bay was a beautiful place. I have since learned some worrying facts about it as it becomes home to First Nation teenagers who need to attend High School, usually many miles away from their remote reserves in Northern Ontario.

Depression, mental health issues, and high suicide rates are such a sad consequence of these young folk being so far away from home at such a tender age.

It marked a milestone in our journey as the first stop in Ontario, and I hope it marks a place for better times ahead for those living here. Oh Canada! Why, oh why, is there such disparity between communities?

We continued on through the vast province of Ontario, ever eager to encounter some of the French-speaking communities we had heard about.

I found the difference between the Saskatchewan and Ontario landscapes both profound and charming. While the prairies offer a sense of freedom and being-at-one with the land and the sky by its openness, Ontario felt like a hug, in tree-form. Trees and rocks loomed up on each side, impossible to tell if anyone actually lived there! I loved it!

January 2, 2017

Hi Family!

Tonight I type, rather wearily, from an odd little chalet in New Liskeard, so close to the Quebec border that most of the people we meet are French-speaking.

Lucy started the day for us at 5:00am, throwing up because she had not drank enough the day before (no big surprise). We have spent the day being ogres to her (and the other three) to keep them all hydrated. Honestly, it seems the more we try the harder they resist! Bloody children.

We finally got here after another twelve hours on the road. We got stuck in the snow on a steep slope, and a guy had to bring his tractor to pull us out. He was French-speaking, of course... No, to be fair, his English was very good, and he was really kind.

The weather has been brilliant, and although incredibly long and monotonous, the roads have been just fine.

I had picked up a light supper (some pasta) and breakfast (full-on sausage, bacon, bread, and eggs from home...) to feed us here. No one was too hungry by 10:00pm though, and we spent most of the meal fighting with Lucy over a drink.

The water pressure in the tap is two drips above a dribble... so washing up after that monster breakfast will be loads of fun! Our hope is to be back on the road by 8:00 or 9:00am. We have eight hours left to do.

Anyway, my optimism is cast-iron, and I refuse to be defeated by exhaustion, frustration, or children who have shriveled up to the size and consistency of a prune.

Will send next installment when destination is attained and the whole mission is successfully accomplished. All offers of medication for severe eye-twitches are gratefully received.

Love you all loads!

Jo xxxxxxxxx

New Liskeard seemed a bit of a non-event, but it turns out they have some amazing stuff going on... everyone has heard of New Liskeard! Our accommodation may have been a little unorthodox, but the owner was just stellar! We found out we had been overcharged by the online travel company we booked through, and he very generously refunded us the difference, and said we should just book through him directly next time! What a sweetie! I would go there again, and I think I would explore Northern Ontario more too; I have a dear friend in Sudbury, and the opportunity to practice French is fantastic!

We finished the last leg of our journey and arrived at our destination of a temporary home in the town of Durham.

January 4, 2017

Hello All!

Sorry I didn't get to type of our arrival last night. Our lovely new landlord came over to greet us with armfuls of red wine and beer.... so, we like him a lot!

The cabin is wonderful, at least a hundred times better than I was expecting! There are two 'sleeping areas' upstairs. One is a bedroom with two single beds and masses of closet space, that Lucy and Sam are sharing. The other is the landing, which comfortably holds two more single beds, plus a couple of chests-of-drawers. It is a complete wrap-around, 'galley' style landing, so Harry and Josh have that. There is a bathroom with shower up there too.

Downstairs, there's an ample kitchen with plenty of cupboards, dishwasher, fridge/freezer, stove, microwave and a delightful 'plant window' that sticks out like a mini greenhouse! Then, you move into the lounge area, which is about 25' by 15', and contains four large sofas (nice leather ones too!), a 'looks-like' wood burning stove that actually operates on propane and clicks on according to the thermostat, and a heap of very beautiful antique furniture. The dining room completes the circuit, roughly 12' x 8', with a big oval dining table and six chairs. More closet space is by the front door.

An archway leads off between the kitchen and lounge area, through which is a laundry area, a second large bathroom with a huge bath tub, and a double bedroom where Jim and I sleep. You can access the attached garage through the laundry area.

Outside we get the beautiful view of the rescue horses Sven owns and keeps here on his farm. Their fencing seems to run right under our windows... the children are just thrilled!

At the back of the living room is a covered deck, which translates to a giant walk-in freezer at this time of year!

The cabin is a timber frame construction, with exposed beams all over the place; it's just lovely!

Today we will finish unpacking the trailer, (I bought a chest freezer full of our own food, which will go in the garage) and all the furniture we bought, thinking there wouldn't be much here! (Definitely considering leaving our guffy stuff and instead trying to pack Sven's antique collection when we leave!)

My plants survived, mostly, with just a tad of frost bite on some of their leaves; they seem happy in their new little window-box spot!

So, we are happy and settled, and indeed in no rush to get back into the bus anytime soon!

So I'll sign off, and perhaps write again in a few days.

Loads of love to all!

Jo xxxxxx

So we settled into life in Durham (not the county, just the town). As in every place we have ever lived, we found friends. It is hard to describe my time there. I loved it immensely, but found I couldn't cope. Waldorf is a different system, very faculty led, without any hierarchy in theory. But it is just theory, and the faculty had its own hierarchy, even if we chose not to recognize it. I worked my behind off to be the best teacher I could be, and bring my gifts to the school.

Our temporary landlord was wonderful, as was his friend

Martin, who visited frequently. They were a hilarious tag-team of constant humour, and loved red wine!

Durham itself was magnificent, as were the surrounding areas. Rivers, lakes, forest… and the houses were so beautiful made of brick, stone, wood, or a combination of all three. I could have settled there, even without the career I had intended for myself, but life takes its own path sometimes.

Jim came-and-went several times, and was absent from our lives for long stretches at a time. He still had livestock back in Saskatchewan to deal with, and the farm to sell. On reflection, I think 'single-parenting-it' for those stretches of time also didn't help and compounded my feelings of inadequacy and anxiety.

March 3, 2017

Hello Family!

I have completed my first two months of teaching!

Despite a number of successes, not least our first week of cooking snacks to feed the whole school daily ('Red Lobster' style biscuits, pancakes for Shrove Tuesday, mini pizzas, and then cheese and onion scones), I still seem to operate on a rotation of dread (every morning), frustration (intermittently throughout the day), and exhaustion (the minute I get home... sometimes even before then!)

I alternate between believing it's simply a very hard road to travel, and I'll "get there" in the end, and deciding I can't do it and I should just quit.

Mostly I defer to the first option. Still, my morning routine usually involves mentally drafting my letter of resignation...

Next weekend is my first training opportunity. I will drive down to Toronto right after school on Thursday to hear a keynote speaker in the evening. All day Friday and Saturday morning are workshops. I have arranged a local B&B accommodation with a kind couple (she is also attending the Friday). I hope it inspires me to keep going! (Still clutching your words mum, "The only way is forward!")

I took the leap and registered for the July three-week residential schooling, that forms the first part of my three year part-time Waldorf Teacher Training.

(Giving courage to my conviction of deferring to that first option!)

Yesterday, I had to do a physical restraint on a student. It was the first time since Kelliher school's delectable delinquent (if you can remember that story?) I managed okay but it added to frazzling the last of my already fried nerves!

With the verbal fisticuffs between our board members (a parent group), it is not difficult to see why some children have such horrendous behaviours! Yet our job is to produce academic excellence and solid strength of character...!???

Do I sound pissed off?

Jim plans to drive out once again in our newly acquired vehicle this weekend. With luck, he'll get here Tuesday.

We still have no news on our farm sale, or farm purchase.

The valuation Jim organised came back quite favourable; friends of ours are interested, and may make us a decent offer if we're lucky. Auctioning the farm off may be another option too.

The farm animals will go to the neighbour who babysat them through January for us. She's working on a fair price to offer for them.

The bees (currently 'sleeping' their way through winter) will probably go to a fellow who has had a couple of chats with Jim and is really interested in them. Jim hopes to split the hive so that he can keep some of the drawn comb (where the bees already built their little honeycomb houses), for when he is ready to start again here.

Of course, with my endless struggles and worrying, he understandably feels reluctant to make any final sales of anything!

Still, even if I don't hold out with this teaching job, I still would like a change of scenery in life. Ontario is so pretty!

I am appreciating a statement Lucy came out with a couple of weeks ago: "I have seen too much; my eyes hurt!"

The toll of educational intensity!

Much love to you all!

Mum/Jo xxxxx

It was beyond hard, and I felt my zeal fading fast. I was at this point still pretty determined to try and make the best of things. The universe seemed to have other ideas though. Our farm did end up going for auction and did not make anything close to what we were hoping to get for it. Such is life.

March 11, 2017

Hello Family!

I am at the beginning of a much-needed two-week break!

I drove down to Toronto on Thursday afternoon, right after my school day ended.

I had scribbled directions and a map (the wrong map, of course!)...

Maybe I was too tired... maybe I just hate driving... maybe I can't read...

I missed an important turn in the spaghetti-junction of outer-Toronto highways. In trying to retrace my footsteps (impossible with the spaghetti!), I just got more and more off track. I pulled over, had a good cry, and resorted to Google Maps to get me going again.

I'd lost a half hour, and only just made it in time to register and find a seat for the keynote speaker. She wasn't very good.

There was some good content though, and afterwards I did manage to find my way to the house I had arranged to stay at, about 15 minutes away.

The couple were kind and friendly. I showered and went straight to bed.

Up early the next morning, I tried to work their unusual toaster, and managed to set off all the smoke alarms (smooth, Joanne).

I was back in the conference by 8:30am. I was beginning to feel quite out-of-sorts, and despite a very enjoyable Waldorf puppet show, one interesting lecture, and one utterly dull-and-boring lecture (gosh the difference it makes if a person cannot speak well publicly!), I really felt like I just wanted to leave.

The workshop I was assigned to started out badly, (I was late after not even being able to read the building layout map we had been provided) but did improve dramatically enough to make me think it wasn't a completely wasted trip.

I learned about integrating Skills and Stories to bring forth Human Capacities. This is the bedrock of Waldorf education, and much of the discussion in my workshop was both valuable and interesting.

My colleague and I met up at the end of the day, 3:30pm, to drive home together in my car... except the electronic key wouldn't work.

It had turned bitterly cold, and a storm-like wind was whipping up. We went inside thinking perhaps the battery needed replacing. Where is the battery on these things anyway?

Our Waldorf teacher trainer was in the hallway, and told us there is a metal key inside the electronic device for occasions like this when technology goes horribly wrong. Hooray, we found a key! Could I drive with this key? Was there even a key hole in the electronic ignition? (My loathing for all things electronic and technologically-advanced is now increasing exponentially with every passing second.)

We tried the key in the driver's door; it didn't open. We tried the key upsidedown. We looked for a key hole in the passenger side door. We even looked at the boot (trunk for non-British readers).

Back inside again, I called CAA (like RAC/AA). My colleague called her husband to come pick us up.

I decided I'd had enough and very much needed to "just go home". Perhaps CAA could come and fix the car/tow me back/burn the car...

My colleague's husband arrived and we went through all of the above processes again. Then, my colleague commented on how she had lost her key, just the same as mine, and wanted to find it to see if she could locate her battery compartment...

I checked in my bag... yes, there was a second, identical, electronic key. I had been using hers, which we summized must have fallen out of her purse and into my bag on our drive in that morning.

I drove to their house, collected my overnight things, updated my scribbled notes to get back on the spaghetti highways, and left.

I missed the first important turn... (you know the script by now I think?)

Finally, making it out of Toronto, I still felt slightly inspired by my training. I planned to continue my Waldorf teaching trajectory, (even if only till June, till grade eight at the most) and put into action all that I had learned.

About an hour and a half into my driving, I missed another important turn. Now on minor roads and in quite heavy snowfall, it took me a while to realise I was going the wrong way.

(The script is now taking on the characteristics of a chorus, don't you think?)

Google Maps took me down sideroads, which it interestingly pronounced "siddy-road", that no man had traveled in quite some time.

The snowfall was now full-on blizzard.

Sod inspiration! I planned to quit the minute I got back to the cabin. We will buy an R.V. and homeschool the children like a roving gypsy family. Skills, Stories, and Human Capacities be damned! I don't care! I should never have been born!...

After three and a half hours of driving, I arrived home.

This morning we have no water. The blizzard and sudden temperature drop have frozen our pipes.

Here are my pearls of wisdom from my experiences these last few days:

1. If the toaster looks weird, leave it alone.

2. Electronic keys should be banned.

3. Electronic keys escaping the ban and making it into general circulation should have unique identifiers (like the owner's photograph, name, birthweight, and inside leg measurement inscribed indelibly).

4. All maps should be accompanied by written instructions a three-year-old could follow, along with a voice-recording describing step-by-step progress.

5. Water is to be prized above all else, particularly the water that lives in the toilet cistern.

6. There is absolutely nothing wrong with living by candle-light in a cave.

Tons of love to you all!

I'll get over myself eventually,

Mum/Jo xxxxxxx

I ultimately chose to leave that chapter of my life behind. Interestingly, I was invited to do an exit interview. I tried to articulate the disparity between a no-tech learning environment, which I really love, and the full-tech communication expectations between faculty members and parents; very discombobulating! The folks conducting my exit interview just smiled and nodded. Interesting.

We then started fishing about for a real home, and began our search right in the vicinity of that area in Ontario. We found a fantastic spot in Peabody, right in the middle of an Amish community (which I loved!) The house was awfully run down, but being the eternal optimists we are, we saw it as a "project", and were totally smitten by the opportunity.

As events ran their course, it became apparent that the owner really didn't want to sell. He ignored our offer for weeks, and then jacked his price up by a couple-of-hundred-thousand. We had to let it go.

March 19, 2017

Hello Family!

We have journeyed through week one of our two week holiday!

The children swing between cabin fever and associated bad behaviours, and grumbling and griping about travel when we choose to go anywhere.

We looked at another property yesterday (started out as four properties, three were sold/withdrawn within that day!) The one left was quite horrid.

Undeterred, we're off to look at three more tomorrow (assuming no one snaps them up overnight.) A little further afield, but in what looks like a very beautiful part of the province, up towards the Bruce Peninsula.

The Amish place is still my favourite, but the owner really doesn't seem too eager to sell. He hasn't come back to us with a counter offer, and still hasn't even begun to look for a place to move to. Personally I think that one, glorious as it could have been, is a non-starter.

Next week we are rather hoping to make a trip to Niagara Falls. Although only a day trip, we might stay over someplace and meet with my tutor, Hilary, again. Her husband is keen to meet with Jim and talk-all-things-farm.

I have been left the onerous task of feeding classroom

critters. Two aquariums containing axolotl (google them... they're really weird!) They require freshly-butchered live earthworms, some frozen blood worms, and frozen brine shrimp. So, I go in every other day to murder a lumbricus terrestris (earthworm).

I also look after a pair of budgies with the less gory diet of birdseed.

I'll keep you posted on next week's endeavours!

Tons of love to everyone!

Mum / Jo xxxxxx

Hilary was the most fantastic tutor! I accomplished my certification in Anthroposophy because of her dedication and unwavering support. Many times I miss our deep and philosophical conversations.

It was during this break that I made my final decision to quit the Waldorf teaching job. I was going to miss the folks there, and that part of the world, which was lovely, but I made my mind up and felt the weight of the world lifted from my shoulders.

March 24, 2017

Hello Family!

I am at the end of the two-week 'March break', back to school on Monday. My step is a little lighter, as I have formally announced my resignation!

After the ups and many-more-downs of my short time here, I have had to draw the line and decide to walk away. I will remain until June, to see my class through the rest of the year, but I think I can survive that.

Despite the huge sense of guilt, it has been good to come out here to Ontario, and experience a different culture, politics, economy, and landscape. Jim and I are in very serious discussions about relocating to this province anyway; it could be a wise move with the favourable primary-producer consumerism that is far more pronounced here than anywhere else in Canada. (Thanks Gee for the advanced education in Food Sovereignty! It really helped put background knowledge to the reality of living here!)

Simply returning to our Saskatchewan farm is still an option, although personally I'm a bit reluctant for several reasons:

1. I love change and adventure (for those who haven't noticed that already!)

2. As farmers this is a very opportunist area to work in.

3. Our Saskatchewan farm is still in heavy debt. If we sell and down-scale we might fix that somewhat.

4. Finally, I fully anticipate homeschooling the children from now on. (I learned a thing or two

about my own abilities, previously doubted and undervalued!) So it doesn't really matter where we choose to settle (Outer Hebrides? Deepest Darkest Peru?)

Anyway, send me your vibes of peace, strength, and tranquility as I embark on the next three months! It does feel better to know there is now a light at the end of my tunnel.

Thanks for the phone conversations and your much-appreciated support!

Loads of love

Mum/Jo xxxxxxx

We took our Home hunt a little further afield, and headed further east towards Kingston. We met the most animated and enthusiastic real estate agent I have ever known. He showed us what I perceived as My Dream Home, and I demanded we put an offer in right away. There seemed to be an absurd level of sniffers showing up, even as we were there, because of some new goat milk opportunity in the nearby city of Kingston. I suspect it made Jimmy have a little cry all by himself later that evening.

I move too fast sometimes, as I recall our initial move to Canada, or even as I recall how Jimmy and I went from tentative steps in our early dating history (I was a divorcee with three children after all) to marriage and a home together. Sometimes I forget he needs time to adjust.

April 2, 2017

Hello Family!

Never a dull moment here in the White House...

We trotted off east a little after 8 in the morning on Friday. We arrived with only minutes to spare for our first viewing at 1:30pm.

And what a "view" it was. It was just a big muddy field (as in a 150-acre plot with no buildings at all), and raining relentlessly. We looked from the car, declared "that's nice", (with our inside voices shouting that it is waaay too close to the highway) and moved on to viewing number 2.

This house was beautiful! Lots of space, but a very flat, unkempt, narrow stretch of ground that totaled 100 or so acres behind it. The house's 'beautifulness' took it into a new price bracket, sooo... "that's nice"... and onto viewing number 3.

Big house, big land parcel, located slap in the centre of a small town(?), but with problematic tenants, who were currently in some sort of war with the owner over 'who-owns-what'. The owner, by all accounts a bless-her-soul elderly lady of ill health, had moments before taken the property off the market because of the hassle... sooooo... onto viewing number 4.

Ah!!! La pièce de résistance! (say that with your best French accent)

You know how sometimes you just get a "yes" feeling? We got it for the Amish place that we emailed to you ages ago... well, we got it here too!

The house is about 100 years old, needs a new roof and a serious facelift, but is structurally sound, and very spacious. There's 80 acres of really nice mixed terrain, and off a very quiet road in Nowhere-ville, AND, is a short 20 minute drive into Kingston!

We are neck-and-neck with another family though; the price was lowered just this week, so all the city folk are sniffing around... and apparently last week's local new headline is of an impending goat-milk plant opening just north of the area. All those wannabes are angling for a hobby farm to make their millions (Grrr... how dare they!)

Time will tell....

Tons of love to all!!

Mum/Jo XXXXXXXXX

So, here we are finding a new home away from our first 'landing site'. We decided to move near to Kingston, Ontario... but I still have to finish up...

April 15, 2017

Hello Family!

We survived another week! I did my best to make

it a "short" week, by injecting two field trips for my class. Having done our daily cooking for our Business Math, we ended the main block by visiting two local Community-Shared-Agriculture farms. One grew vegetables and herbs for around 20 families, and the other, much larger, for 80 families. All pretty interesting stuff!

Jim was our chauffeur, since vehicle insurance declares I cannot transport my own students during school time. I suspect they are aware of the overwhelming urge your average teacher would experience on such occasions, to drive her entire cargo over the edge of a cliff, just to escape the agony of her remaining teaching career... Fair enough.

We've had some warm sunny days, and the children and Jim have spent time outside, working on the garden, and giving me the much-needed quiet time to finish my thesis for my anthroposophy course, which draws to a close very soon.

I am counting the days until my flight to England!!

In the meantime, I am occupying myself with some odd choices, like agreeing to teach all the grade classes the Maori Stick game for our May Fair Day. Also, I wrote a play for my class called 'Medieval Top Gear', and we are enduring the pain of rehearsals on a regular basis, before our debut performance in early June.

My friend and colleague, Leone, has loaned me the

"easy-peasy, just follow this..." textbook for our next unit in physics. Here is the first lesson: "Have your class listen to silence." Absolute genius... Not! Our main lesson is one and a half hours every day. My class, like most other classes of middle years children, and are unable to respect the golden tones of silence for 3 seconds, never mind an hour and a half!

Even funnier was the second day's lesson where we are supposed to review the activity we did on day one...

Thankfully, I had not put all my trust into the already questionable resources imparted by the school and its staff. I have armed myself with a collection of "Whizz Bang Experiments for Thoroughly Disinterested Children" Volumes 1, 2, and 3, from our local library.

No more news on our imminent move or non-move situation.

Anyway, keep smiling!

Tons of love to all!

Jo xxxxxxxxxx

I still maintain that my time spent at that Country School was an enormous influence on my life today, and gave me a set of memories like no other. Struggle as I did, the integrity, endurance, and pure dedication of others who worked there was impressive. In my emailed correspondence of that time,

I brush a lot of this off, and ridicule the aspects of the job that caused me so much difficulty, but anyone can do that. The true grit of the situation is in the folks who are still there, doing the very thing I couldn't do. You can see my weakness in the episodes that follow; I am not at all Parzival.

I do try my level best to keep my chin-up and my smiles bright, as I fight through further challenges.

April 22, 2017

Hello Family!

Sunshine and Optimism... this is the way to go, I think!

Of course, it's a delusional construct of my own desperation... but hey... whatever! It's another week conquered (I am deliberately replacing my first choice of word "survived" with "conquered" in the true spirit of Sunshine and Optimism...)

There were actually some quite nice moments... in bringing physics to my students, I chose to go with the KISS principal (Keep It Simple, Stupid). I picked a really nice set of library books, probably designed for six-year-olds, but with some very whizz-bang experiments of a kitchen-table calibre.

We had a shaky start with 'experiencing' shadows. My charges, on the very cusp of adolescence in most cases, were not exactly gripped by my trying to persuade them to check-out shadows on the classroom floor. (Go Google "phenomenology". It is the Waldorf approach to science... a tricky beast to master).

This led to a slightly more thrilling experience of After Images. They particularly loved colour after-images. Try this at home (obviously with safety goggles, lab coat, and a crash helmet on). Have a piece of coloured paper and a piece of plain white paper side-by-side. Stare at the colour paper for 30 seconds to a minute perhaps, then look quickly at the white paper... cool eh?

We made fish-in-the-bowl experiments. Just cut out identical fish shapes in different colour paper. Draw a black eye on each fish. Put one fish on a piece of white paper. On a second piece of white paper, draw a big, empty fish bowl. Putting each side-by-side again, stare at the fish eye for 20-30 seconds; then, quickly look at the fish bowl... super cool, eh?

I rode the 'high' of being Successful Science Teacher of the Day... ooh, till about lunchtime, I think!

More sombre accents to the week included the faculty meeting, where it turns out I am pretty much entirely responsible for the imminent collapse of the whole school, just by giving my resignation last month. Who knew?!

A new fight has broken out, this time between faculty members and administration. In true form, the fight was conducted publicly, using email, with half the world copied-in each time. Some of the parents have started cyber-yelling too! The threat of withdrawal of children escalates... (I guess that is my fault too).

Oh, here's something that'll make you laugh. In response to my resignation, faculty requested that parents put forward a list of preferences for future hiring. Here's what the demands are: Someone with 1. a minimum of ten years teaching experience, 2. fully Waldorf qualified, 3. very strong in science and math, and 4. an expert in middle years education.

I nearly spat out my tea! For the pay on offer? Crikey! Throw in a doctorate or two, maybe lifelong membership and service to the Peace Corps! What about a Grammy or an Oscar?

Sorry, not very S&O of me...

Jim and Harry are Saskatchewan-ing it right now. I'm not quite sure what it involves, but the hope is some sort of progress with our sorting/packing/farm sale type of thing.

The auction for our farm ends May 15th, while I'm with you English folk! (OMG Hooray for that glimmer of sanity and happiness!)

We are experiencing rocky ground with the purchase of our new, hopeful Ontario farm. It turns out we stumbled upon a "blinder" of a deal, and now all and sundry are sniffing around, and it looks mighty likely we'll be 'gazumped'.

Still, S&O to the fore. I am utterly... (okay, slightly...) convinced that the karma of the universe will prevail, and I have nothing to worry about. If not this proverbial fish, another will swim right by.

Do you see how my new S&O brain is working? (I'm into my second glass of red wine; it's 1:30pm; and I've skipped lunch).

My positive outlook consists of waiting for Jim and Harry's return, which will bring Geena for a lovely three-night visit before her outward bound flight! Hooray!!

Loads of love to you all,

Mum/Jo xxxxxx

My resignation did indeed cause a stir. I was subjected to a rather humiliating process of accusatory emails being read aloud to each and every faculty member as they entered our meeting room, in their various stages of delay. It's no way to treat a person. I knew I had made the right decision, although there was still a sadness to leaving what I had truly believed to be "the holy grail of teaching."

May 26, 2017

Hello Family!

My highlight this week is collecting Geena from Durham this evening! We are trying out the local 'Air Bus' system that transports 'arrivals' around Ontario.

I'll let you know her opinion of it. She should be at our local Tim Horton's by 8:00pm.

We are down to three weeks of school. Things continue to be pretty rough. My friend and colleague, Lily, has made the decision to leave the school also, and the remaining staff have really turned on her. I am trying to support her as we finish up the year, but the pettiness of this place really defies belief!

Last night I fielded a phonecall from a parent, who was worrying over raffle tickets lost, and her son's feeling that I was mad with him. I assured her I wasn't. I was, in fact, trying to highlight the difficulties/annoyance of raffle tickets. I can remind children every day, but I can't do any more than that!

An hour later I get a second call from one of the school's administrators, and a good telling-off for sending tickets home with children. Apparently, I wasn't supposed to as they were only for me to sell! (Who knew?!)

Another good cry and and several glasses of wine.

Note to self: buy new batteries for crystal ball in order to understand what other people expect of me, without choosing to tell me.

Jim left us 6:00am Wednesday morning. He is back in Saskatchewan trying to arrange our impending relocation.

Tons of love to all

Mum/Jo xxxxxxxxx

The last stretch at school was tricky, but I am still in touch with some of my friends from that time. It was only a few months after our move that dear friends came all the way from Durham to Kingston to stay with us for a weekend, and we still write!

June 4, 2017

Hello Family!

Hope you are all well and happy!

We are getting closer and closer to our Big Move date! We relinquish possession of our Saskatchewan farm on June 15th, just two weeks away! Jim has organized the hire of a big U-Haul truck, and has also bought a great big tow-trailer. He will drive both, loaded-up to the nines, in a fortnight's time.

We expect to meet around the area of Barrie (Ontario) once he gets there, and we'll convoy it over to Kingston, dropping off the trailer at our new farm, and returning the U-Haul to a dealership.

We'll drive back here to Durham, and Jim will fly back to Saskatchewan one more time to bring his pick-up truck (that is, if the first load contained everything. If not we'll all drive back to collect the rest... a prospect I am not looking forward to!!)

We gain possession of our new place on June 30th.

We are expecting a much simpler lifestyle, concentrating on farming produce that can be sold locally. I may investigate a return to working with grown-ups in the educational field, making the most of our nearby University City. This will all have to fit around homeschooling of course!

Jim has done a stellar job of getting rid of tons of accumulated detritus! Neighbours have bought equipment, steel stock, furniture, livestock... and been offered 'buy one get one free' deals in most cases!

We chat every day, and have laughed, cried, and negotiated through all sorts of trials and tribulations (mostly mine), and ideas and innovations (mostly his). We've decided which light fittings to trade-out so that we can keep our favourites. Discussions have occurred over whether or not we should take the big steel sink. What about the 'fire escape' steps?

It's a new and exciting chapter that helps me shift my focus away from my current situation, and reminds me that this phase is almost at its end. Phew!

With tons of love to all!

Mum/Jo xxxxxxxxxx

Well, I don't want to dwell too much on the despair of my

situation there, but it gives a person an idea of why we moved to our place at Perth Road, Ontario.

July 4, 2017

Hello Family!

I am in a library in Kingston sending a quick email to let you know all is well!

We hope to have our new landline installed by July 17th (quite a wait I know!), and we currently have no cell phone coverage and no internet... "Boo Hiss," said the children!!

The house is spectacular! The children have a bedroom each, and although some pretty extreme 'facelifting' is required, it's all very serviceable right now.

We've unpacked half the kitchen equipment, and have a lovely (very old, in mustard yellow) working fridge/freezer, stove, and dishwasher.

We found a bat on the staircase to the attic... gulp! We are debating how best to deal with this as we plan to renovate up there, and replace the roof. We don't want any nutty environmentalists forcing us to live with bat colonies! I suspect "Silence is Golden"!

Anyways, loads of love to you all!

Mum/Jo xxxxx

It was an utterly gorgeous, century farm house, with around 70-plus acres of rock, tree, and a little bit of pasture. Man, I loved that property!

One of the biggest features was meeting the person to whom the property had been attached for three generations. He lived just down the road. The connection was instant. He had grown up in that house, and his parents had bought it from his grandparents who built it way-back-when. We learned the stories and the history, and these folks helped us map our way forward both with the house and in the community.

He died tragically and suddenly after we'd been there six months. For one of our sons, just about twelve years old, it was his first experience of loss and grief. His wife and I remain good friends, sharing phonecalls and planning future visits. I love her like a sister.

We joined the local church right away (this has always been a thing we do; I cannot recommend it enough!) Perth Road United Church served us and we served it as much as we possibly could, and we made some fabulous friends there.

October 24, 2017

Other news, in brief: We looked at local schools. Lucy may go into French Immersion next September. Harry may go into a local high school. I still don't have a paid job, but I am enjoying my volunteer hours at our local community centre. (I do a half day in the kitchen, a couple hours in the community garden, and this week I began some time with the seniors who attend an adult day programme.)

The kids now have weekly music lessons with our next door neighbour, an utterly brilliant Music Director in the Kingston City Lutheran Churches. (She also has commented on Sam's music genius).

Our home-schooling is going well. Aside from daily math, English, music and occasional French, we are heavy on 'home renovations' learning opportunities. (Hahahaha!) Harry has joined me for a couple of my gardening volunteer hours, where other school kids come to help in the community garden and food bank. It's a good networking opportunity for him.

I still can't make homebrew as fast as I can drink it.

I learned the most beautiful leaves in September belong to the Sumac tree with every shade from lemon-yellow, to peach, orange, and fire-red!

Can't tell you how much I love you all!

Mum/Jo xxxxxxxxxx

I was full throttle trying to establish a life at our Perth Road residence. We loved everything about the place. One of the enticing factors about moving that far east was knowing I was so much closer to England, just one solitary flight, in fact. But the reality was that apart from that one, short weekend back in Durham, I never travelled to England again. The advantage was wasted. Still, I kept up that optimism and persevered with any and every avenue or opportunity I could think of, including a return to full time education and post-graduate studies.

March 5, 2018

Hello All!

Thought I'd share a quick update...

My application to Queen's University to study for a PhD has been officially rejected.

The Professor, bless him, undertook the onerous task of calling me in person this afternoon to let me know. They have suggested I apply to do a Masters in Environmental Science, as a potential pathway to a future doctorate. Since I already have a Masters (in 'science'... light years different to 'environmental science' apparently), I will decline.

Amongst the obvious, crushing disappointment (said tongue-in-cheek), I feel rather relieved, if I'm honest.

Whilst my part-time, cape-wearing self dogmatically insists that four years of full time study, with a "nice-little-earner" part time job on the side, juggling children, home, farm, food, and laundry would be a total breeze.... a substantial part of my inner psyche (the bit wearing comfy shoes and a cardigan instead of a cape, debating the gargantuan issue of another cup of tea being wise when faced with a 15-minute, no-toilet-option journey to the next town) suggests this may have been A Narrow Escape in the grand scheme of things!

So, for as long as I can possibly manage to, I will swear-off formal education. I am 47, next stop 50... perhaps I could retire entirely from thinking?

Or perhaps I could put my thinking into more practical applications, instead of endless study.

Watch this space, as I grow multiple trays of veggie seedlings on the dining table, contriving with Jimmy ways to build, heat, and irrigate a greenhouse WITHOUT POWER!

Go ahead and 'Google' (although officially a verb these days, I am in rebellion and insist on inverted commas) a Jean Pain Mound... add to that a wonderful sloping, rugged landscape, and a bit of imagination with water run-through management, and voilà!

Also, I am quite tired.

Before I leave you, here's a bit of hilarity I'd like to share... 'Google' "The One Ronnie: My Blackberry Doesn't Work". It is the surviving Ronnie Corbett, with Harry Enfield, making a total mockery of our technological age.

"PAH!" to technology, to academia, to pollution, and to the disease of western consumerism. I am sticking with seeds and soil! Hurrah!

Tons of love to you all!

JO xxxxxx

The 'facelift' turned out to be very extensive renovations through a really great local construction company. So remarkable was our home at the end of it all that I can still find pictures of it today on the internet, showcasing such elements as the steel roof tiles.

HEADING WEST

It crept up slowly at first, and I chose to keep ignoring it. Our older children travelled out by plane, train, and automobile to visit, but not very often. I travelled back to Saskatchewan, too, in preparation for my first grandchild's arrival. I was also there in the delivery room the day he arrived! The realisation that I needed to go back eventually overwhelmed me, and in a tearful tsunami of emotion I blurted out to Jimmy that we had to move.

It was pretty much the same story as when we left the Prairies, but in reverse. This time we had one-shot at packing everything up, or so we thought. In truth, Jimmy got to do a second trip a few months later, but we didn't know that was going to be the case when we piled almost all of our possessions into a large U-Haul van and a trailer. The "almost" is because we ran out of space, and also ran out of steam.

I remember the event almost like a nightmare. I had spent weeks packing up the house, ordering the string of events so that everyone had a bed to sleep in and clothes to wear right up until the last minute. The barn and work shops fell to Jimmy though, and bless him, he became overwhelmed. So much had been parked out there; so much stashed in boxes.

Our trip was planned to accommodate the bees and the plants more than to accommodate us. I dug up all the perennial plants we had ordered and paid for, thinking this would feed our bees here in Ontario for years. They got bagged, bundled, or potted into anything remotely suitable, and loaded into the back of the pick-up truck.

I remember my day lilies were hanging-out from a clear-plastic-garbage-sack that was precariously lodged inside our old carriage pram from the UK, all locked down in the bed of that pick-up truck, along with our beehives, which were each wrapped in plywood frames to try and contain the bees. The plywood didn't work too well though. At each gas station stop there was a small cluster of bees clinging to the strapping that secured the hives.

We worked until it was too dark to work, trying to liberate and pack each category of hardware from the quonset, the "paint" shed (the family who originally owned the place were antique dealers and furniture restoration folk), and the barn. (Man, was that barn glorious. It was HUGE! Two stories and full of remnants from former times and who-knows-where-else.) It was too much.

We had engaged in a friendship with some local antique dealers. We met them through a social-media training course we embarked on because of a provincial grant we had been awarded, by happenstance. We invited our new friends to come evaluate and take whatever they deemed appropriate from the top floor of our enormous barn, resplendent with artifacts of old. We had some takers less willing to compensate for their treasure, too. Our antique-oriented friends helped us out long after our departure, bless them.

July 15, 2019

Hello Family and Friends!

Well, we made it!

We spent approximately 45 hours on the road... made all the more challenging after spending Friday furiously packing until midnight, with a catch-up 3:00am start on Saturday. We eventually drove away at 7:00am!

The children were fantastic. Harry in particular worked tirelessly.

Jim drove the big 26' U-Haul, with a large covered trailer behind. I drove the pick-up truck, with our new tipping trailer in tow (and managed to avoid any reversing for the whole 45 hours!)

We got as far as Hearst when Jim's trailer tire blew out... neither one of us realized, and Jim drove on the rim for a few miles before we pulled in for fuel. Oops!

Luckily, we not only had a spare wheel for the trailer, but my super-clever husband had the forethought to pack a full puncture-repair kit, including two heavy duty jacks, at the very last in the U-Haul. Half an hour later we were off again! Hooray!

Two hours later the spare wheel blew out.

By now it was 11:00pm, and we had pulled into a truck stop, too exhausted to safely drive much further. Realizing the tire situation, we quickly decided we were going nowhere right now.

We cancelled the motel we had booked in Thunder Bay (a further three hours driving), and we just hunkered down in our vehicles as best we could for a few short hours. I recommend that you NEVER do this. It was absolutely vile!

At 5:00am we called out-of-hours "OK Tire", and by 6:00am we were back on the road, with a brand new wheel and brand new spare.

8:00pm saw the third trailer tire blow out. Thank goodness we bought two new ones!

By now we had reached Winnipeg, and for a moment wondered if we should replace the remaining two wheels... not an option; they will come out for emergency roadside, not cautionary preventative measures.

We took the rest of the journey at a slower pace, with continual prayer to make it. We finally arrived at 1:00am Saskatchewan time (3:00am Ontario time), with all eyeballs on stalks!

Bees have survived and seem happy. My thousand-

and-one plants survived and seem happy. Jim, the children, and I survived, and we seem happy, too.

The house is.... unique. Unique is, I think, the best word ("odd" and "oh dear" are also close contenders).

Cows arrive later this week. We share the yard with the owners, a very friendly elderly couple.

Hope this email isn't horribly long! I'll write more soon.

Mum/Jo xxxxxx

July 27, 2019

Hello!

Our new home has loads of space, and we are so very happy to have the bees with us. The cows finally arrived yesterday. (Looking frighteningly thin after a two-week delay in the holding facility, fed only rationed hay... not our fault; someone else's goof-up, but what can you do?)

Our biggest issue is sulphur and iron in the water... very smelly!

Also, I am still feverishly sending out my CV for a job, since rent needs to be paid.

We inherited a bit of a veggie garden the previous tenants planted, so that's nice, and the raspberry bushes here are vast. The landlord lets us help ourselves!

My well-travelled perennial plants are also doing great... Hooray!

We have a final push to retrieve items that didn't make it onto our initial convoy... the plastic for the hoop house (10' long, 150lb heavy, worth around $900), and the whipple tree for our chain harrows. I know it seems stupid that such things got "forgotten", but there we are. We have found a very reasonable haulage company, so it should work out okay.

We are settling in well though, and really loving our little local town of Lumsden.

Tons of love to all!

Jo xxxxxx

We spent a torturous year at the rental property, waiting for the Ontario farm to sell. Mercifully no one hijacked the purchase of our new property in all that time, and the owners had little choice but to wait the year out with us.

In June, all the paperwork was officially done, and we were able to go and see our new farm for the very first time. We were not disappointed on that visiting day. It was everything we could have hoped for. Disappointment came after we moved in, when we discovered all the fallacious, dubious, and flawed elements of our new home.

What awaits next is a bit of a rinse-and-repeat story, as we have had plans drawn-up and building permits issued for an extensive set of renovations. A person could be forgiven for thinking we have money to burn, but we survive on the solitary wages of a school bus driver right now, with nothing more than a hope and prayer to carry us through the next part of our journey. We are optimists through-and-through, and we have never let a trifling issue such as abject poverty stop us from charging head-first into new adventures and potential bankruptcy.

Aside from the necessary renovations to our home, we have plans to build an attached, sunken greenhouse that will use passive geothermal heat (in addition to heat from our home) to allow year-around growing of a small selection of vegetables and maybe even some dwarf fruit trees. Inflated construction material prices mean this project may be much further into the future than we would like, but the plans have been approved, so technically it is a reality, even if only on paper.

As for the future, I have sworn many oaths to my family that we will stay put. Thus, our farm will be a long-term project, where we may experience not only the hard work of building a working, sustainable farm, but also enjoy the benefits of living with it (rather than running off to start again someplace else).

Only time will tell what happens next, but for now, we are here…and we are happy.

ABOUT THE AUTHOR

JOANNE WHITE is a real farmer, but she became so by marrying Jimmy, who was born and raised on an English dairy farm. She actually grew up in the suburbs of the West Midlands in England with a back garden the approximate size of a dining table.

Jo holds a degree in Biology, a Masters in Science, and teaching degrees from both the UK and Canada. While she has been employed in all these disciplines, she found her vocation in organic farming. With a philosophy to be mindful of whole systems, she is interested in maintaining the integrity of the natural balance of things and to live both with and off the land.

Jo currently lives and works on her and her husband's farm near Lumsden, in Saskatchewan, Canada where they manage and maintain 160 acres of land, various livestock, and bees. They run a stand at local Farmers' Markets selling fresh vegetables, meat, eggs, and honey. They also sell their farm products directly from the farm gate.

For more information, feel free to visit www.jjwhitefarms.com or follow on Facebook @JJWhiteFarmsLtd

Printed in Great Britain
by Amazon

71726475R00125